Adult Coloring Book

Stress Relieving Patterns

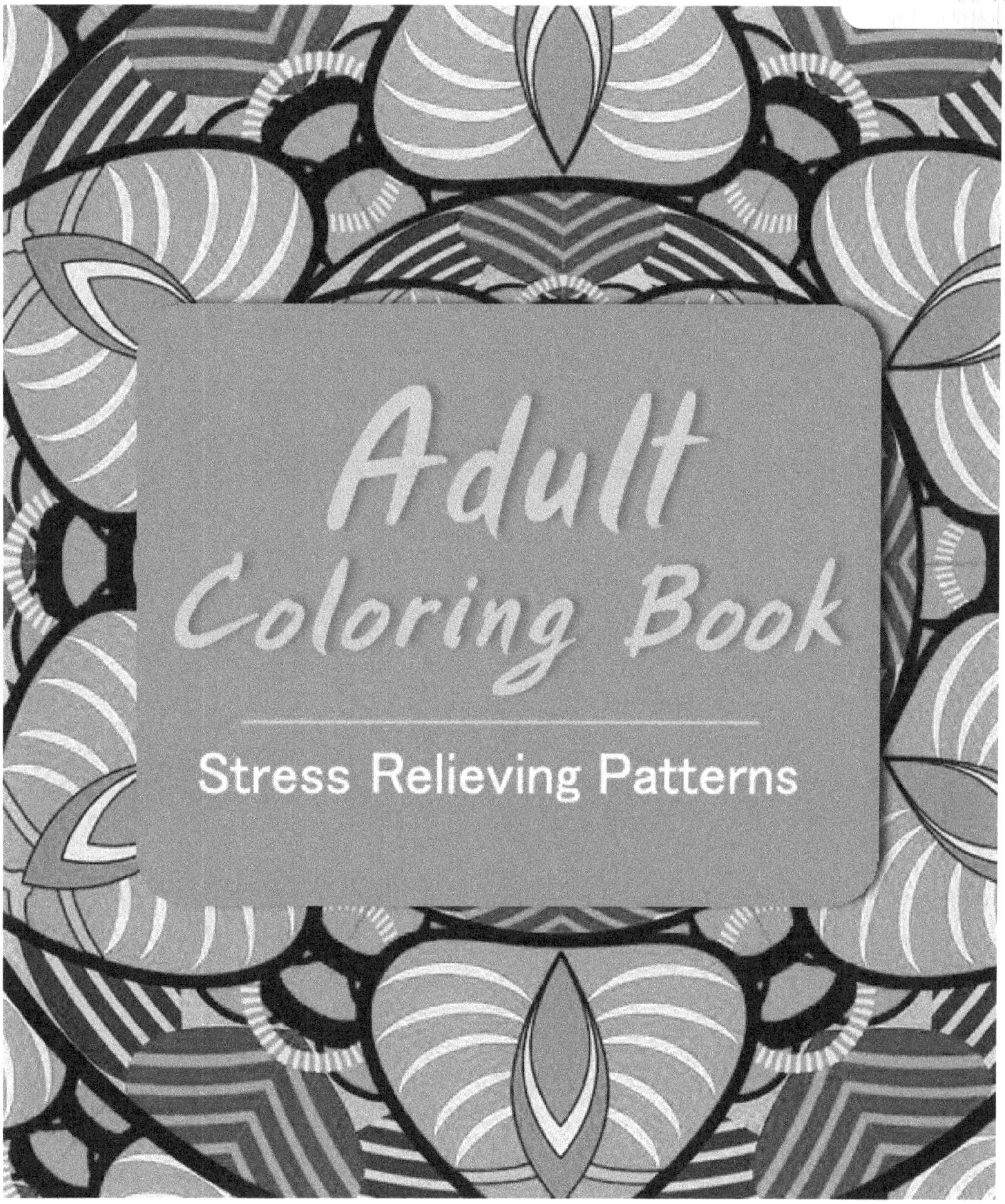

Vol. 15

V ART™

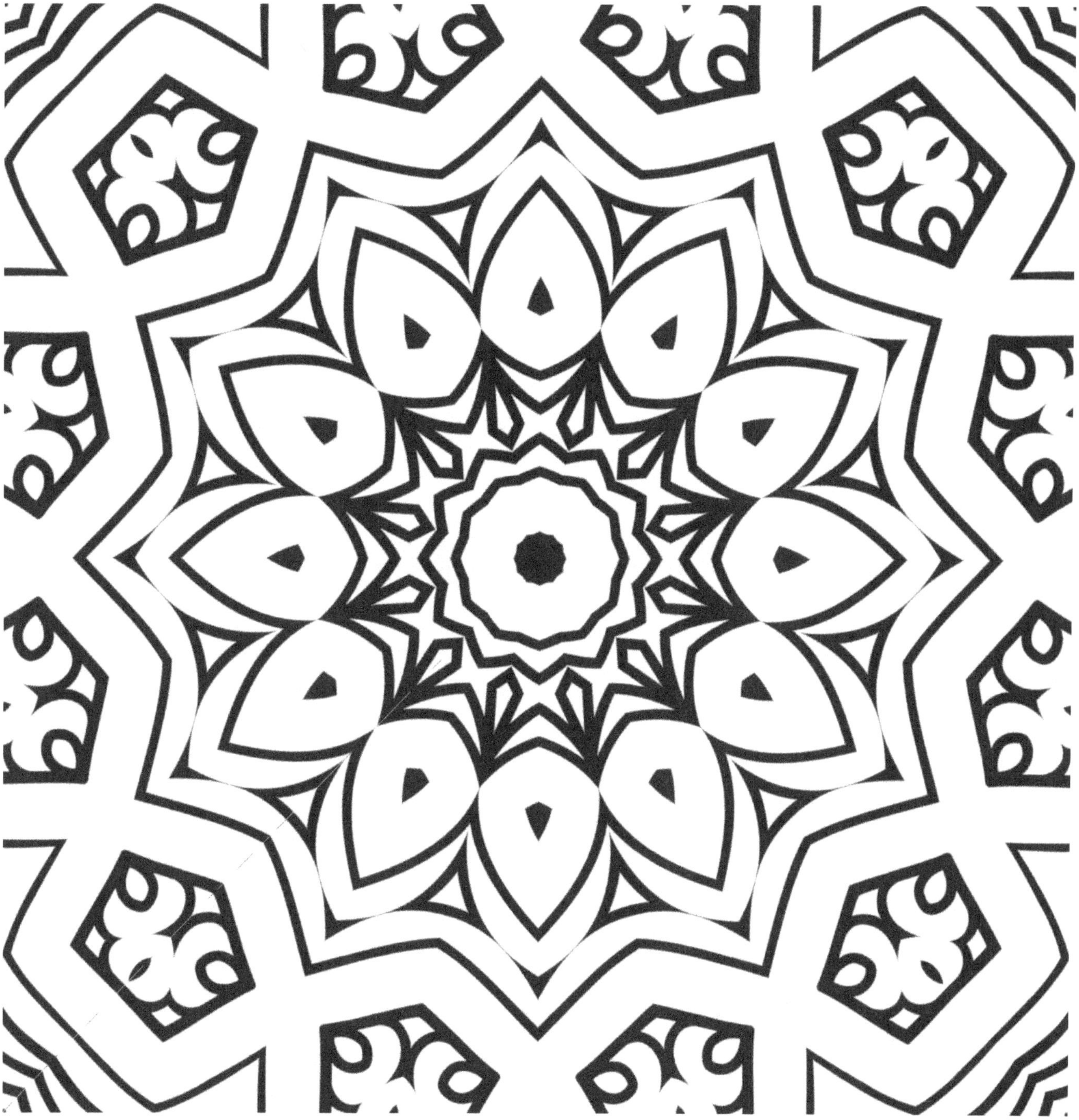

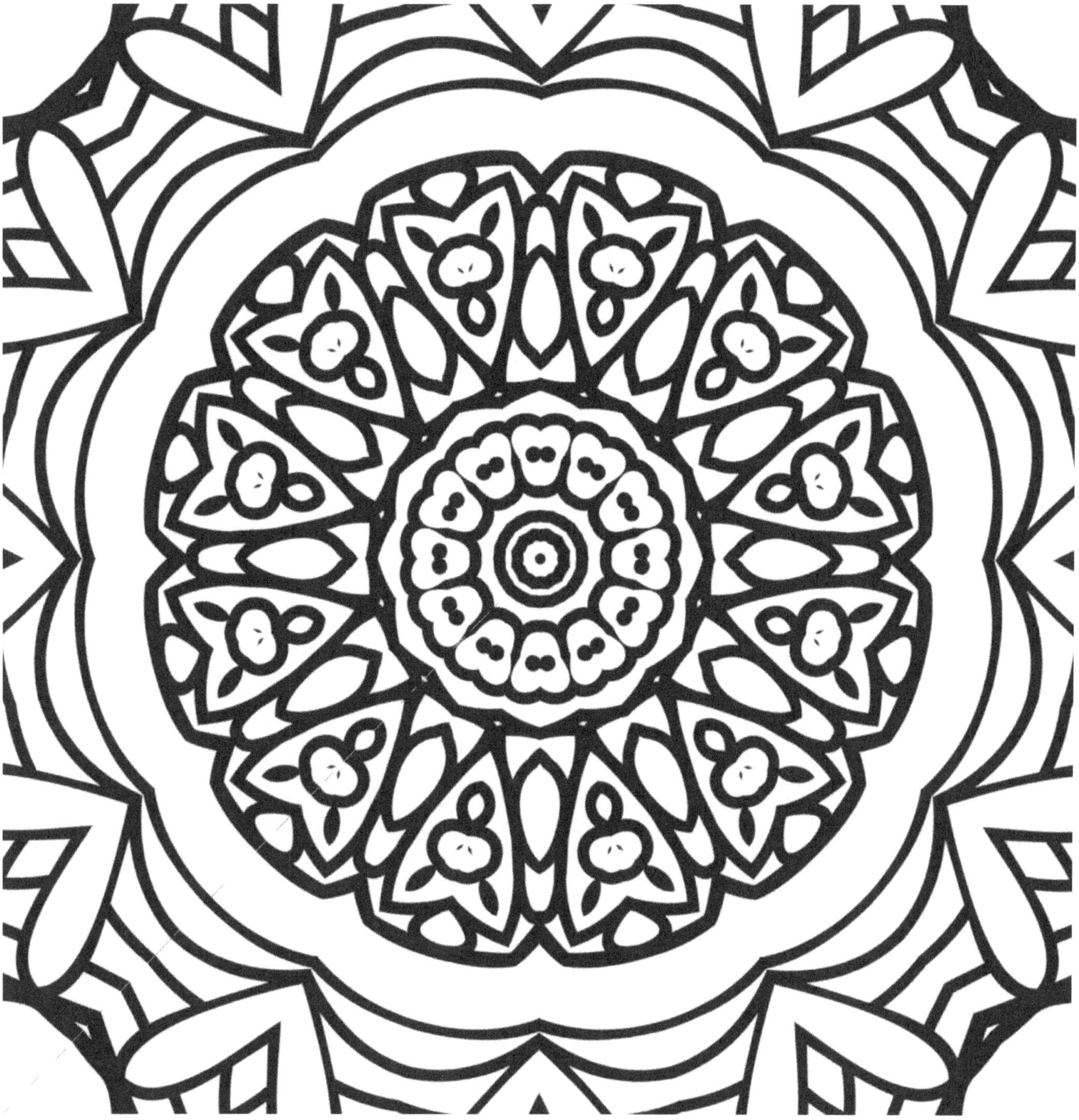

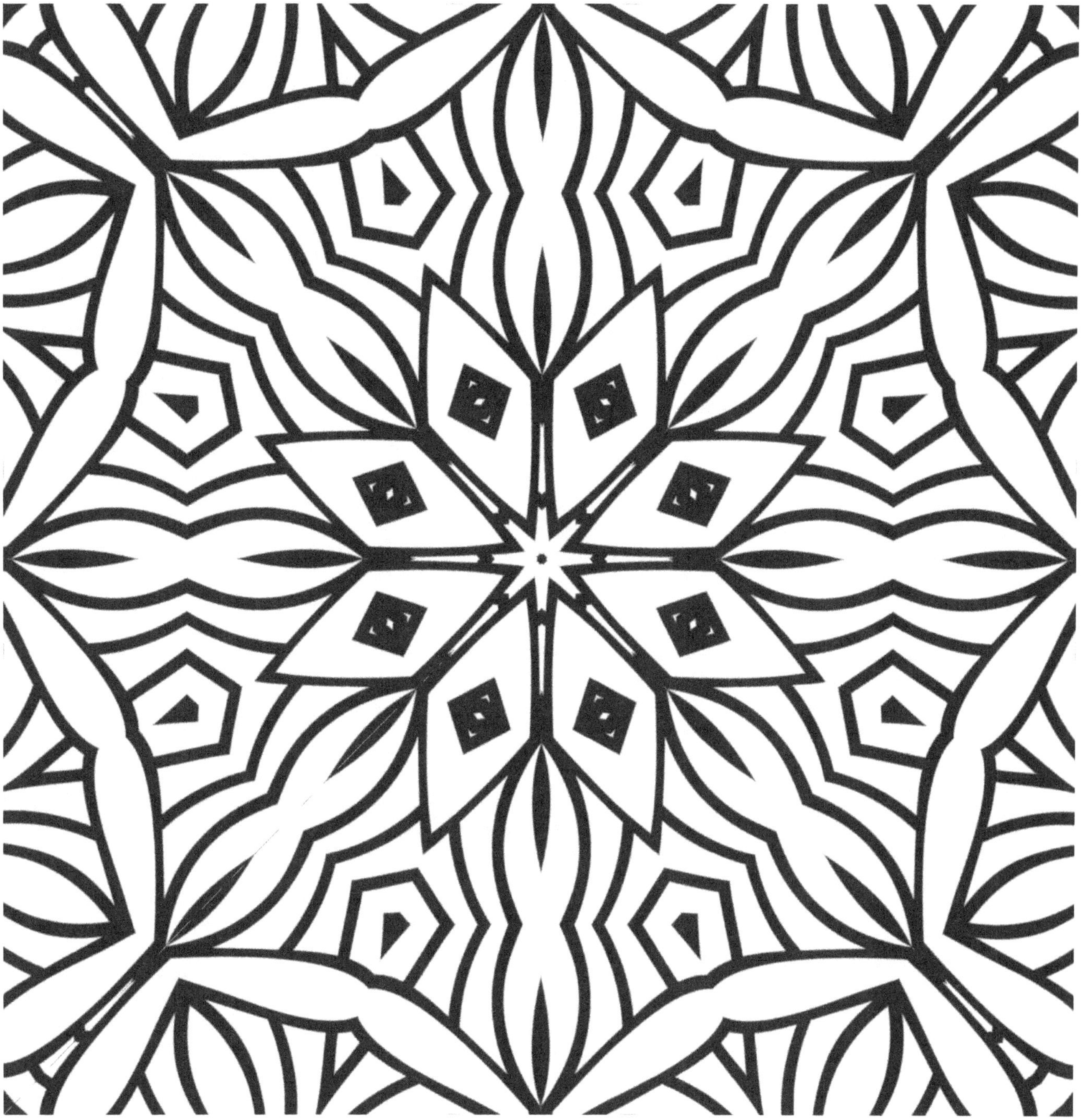

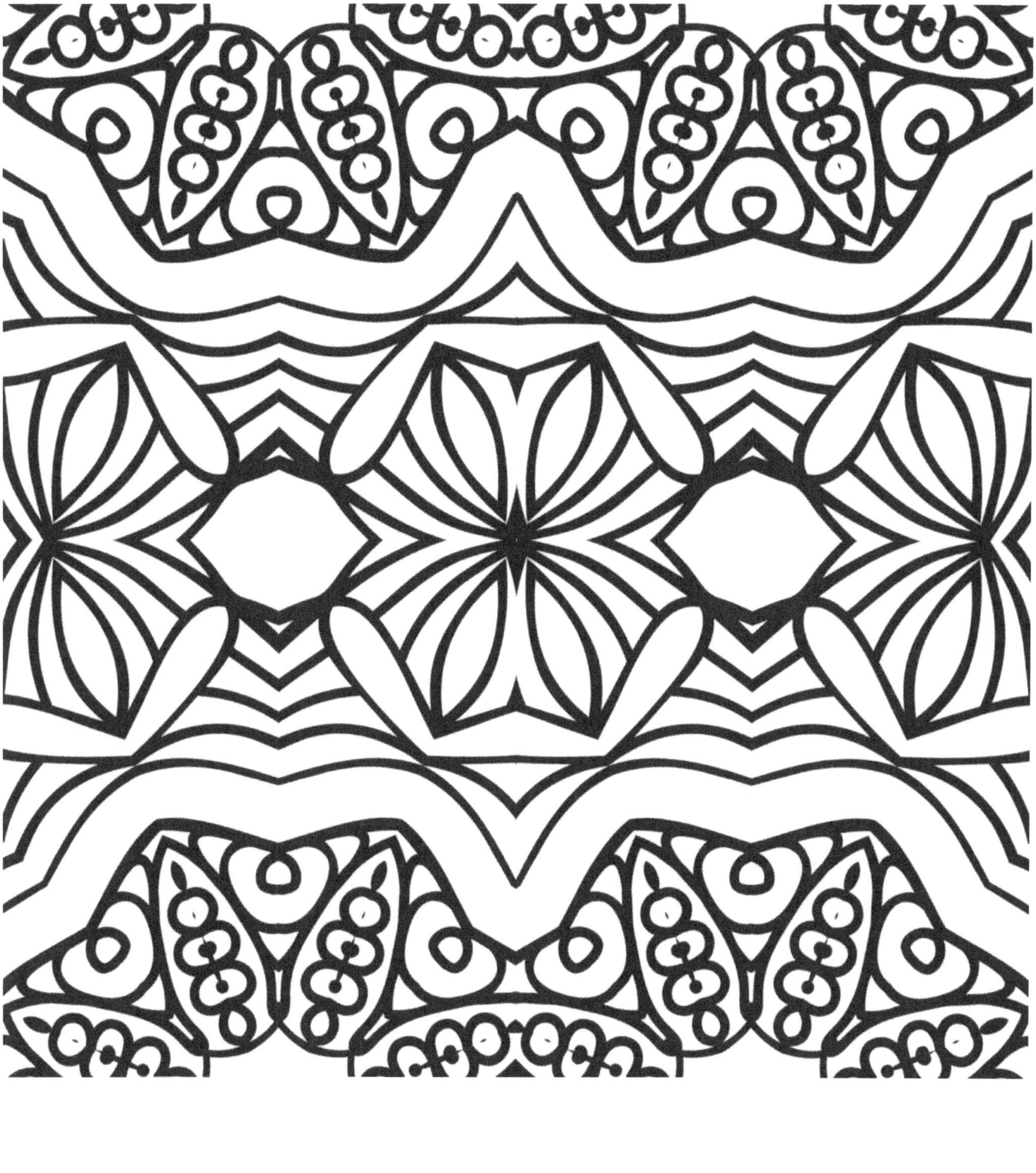

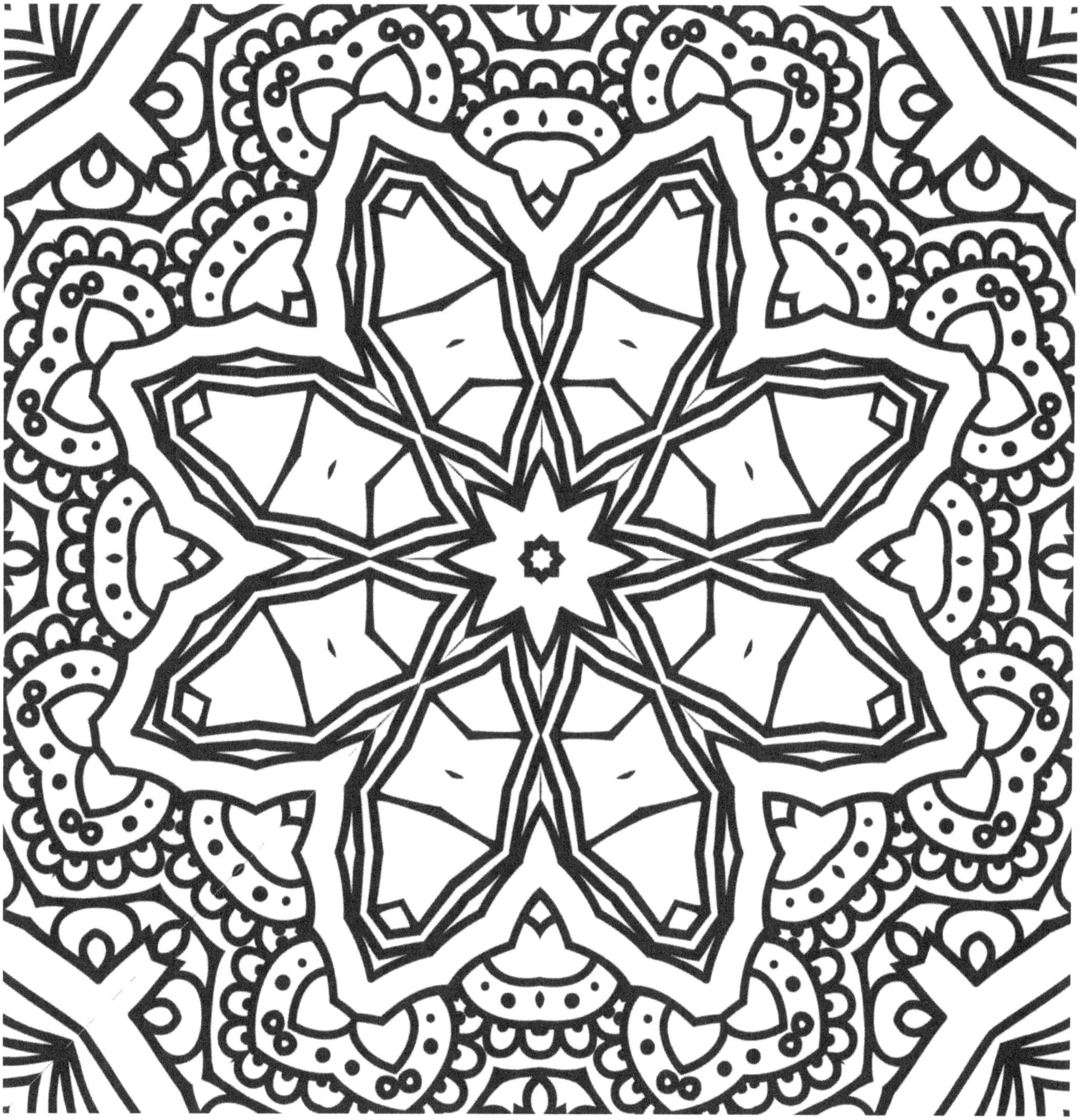

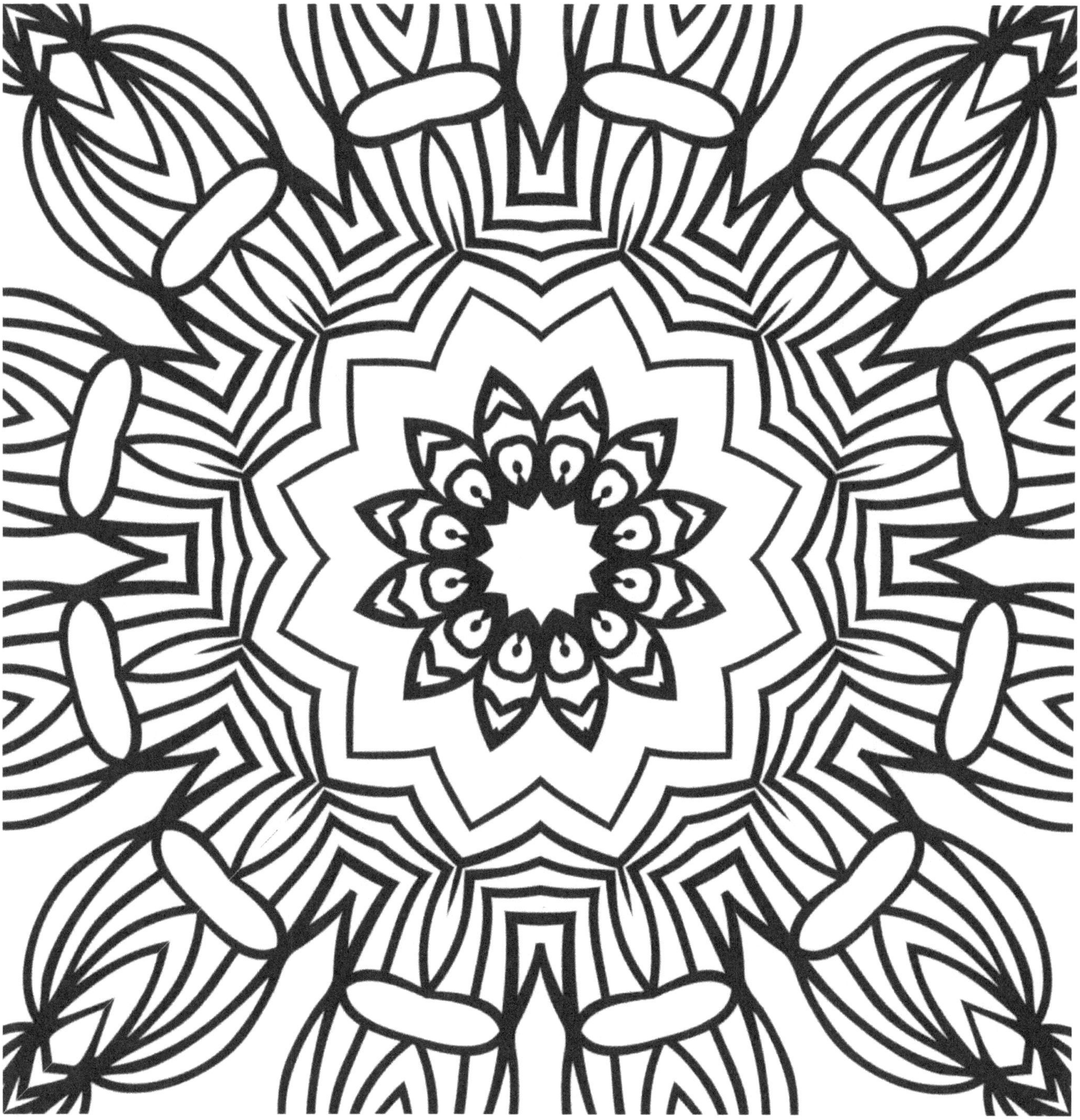

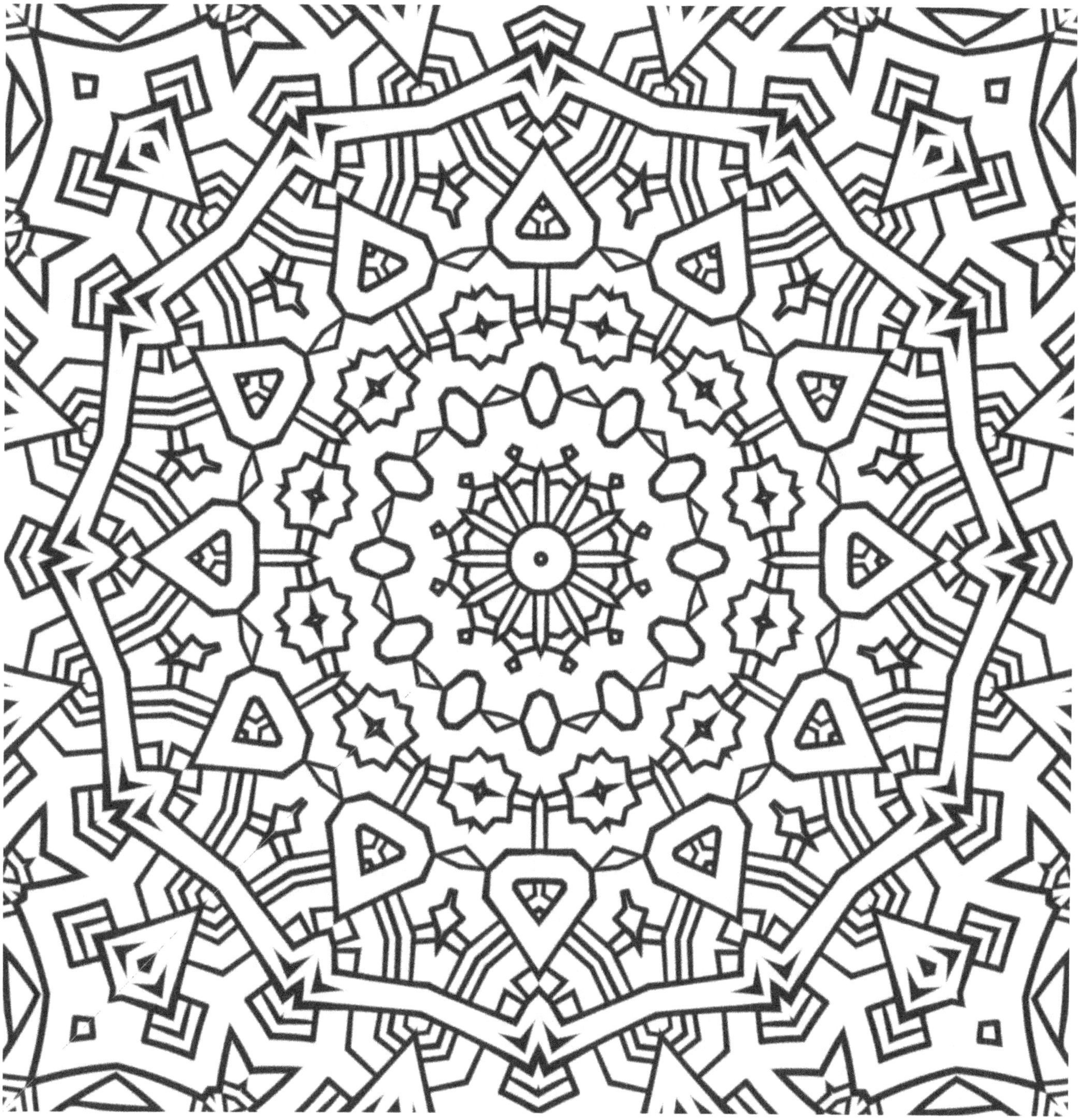

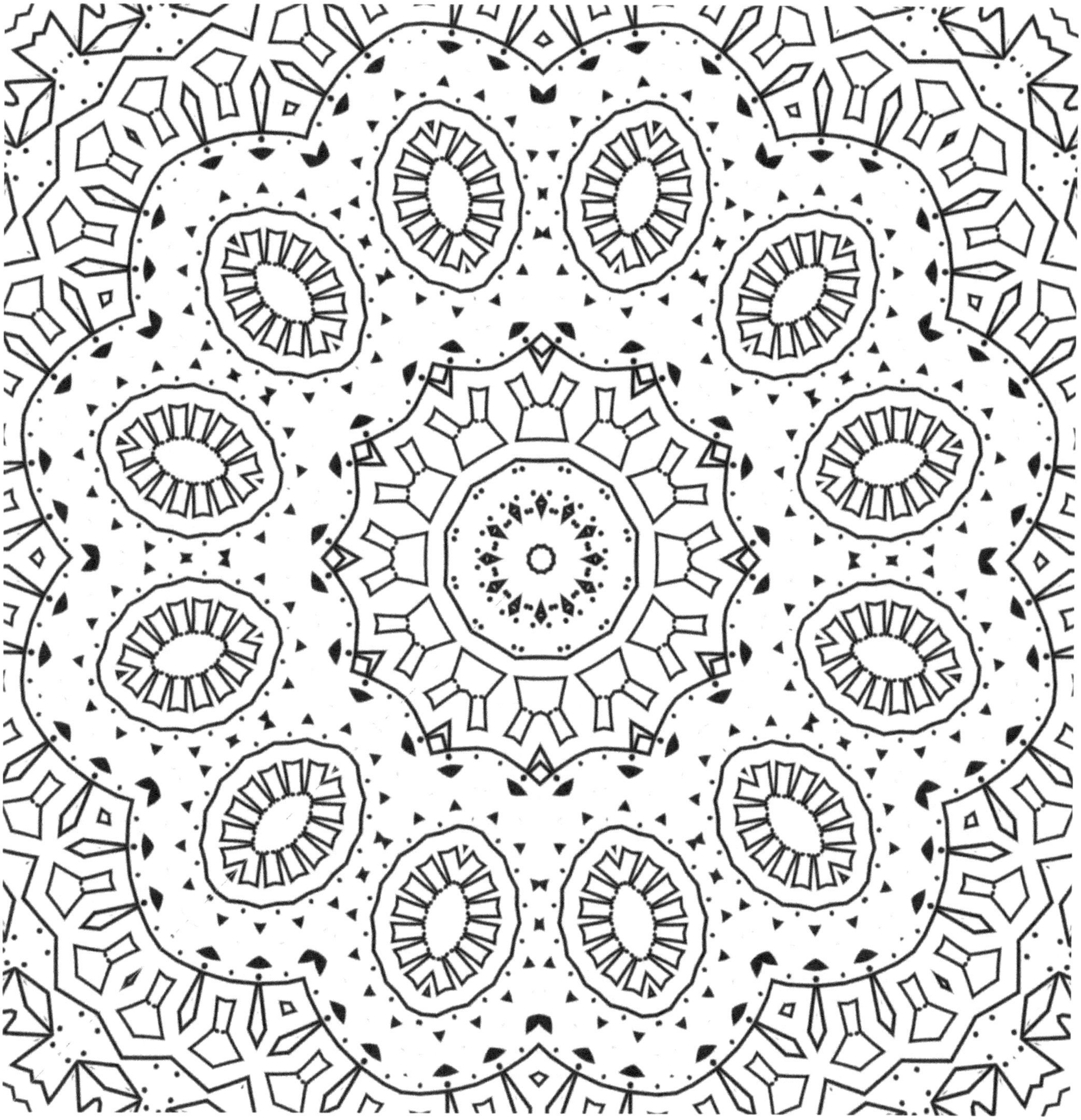

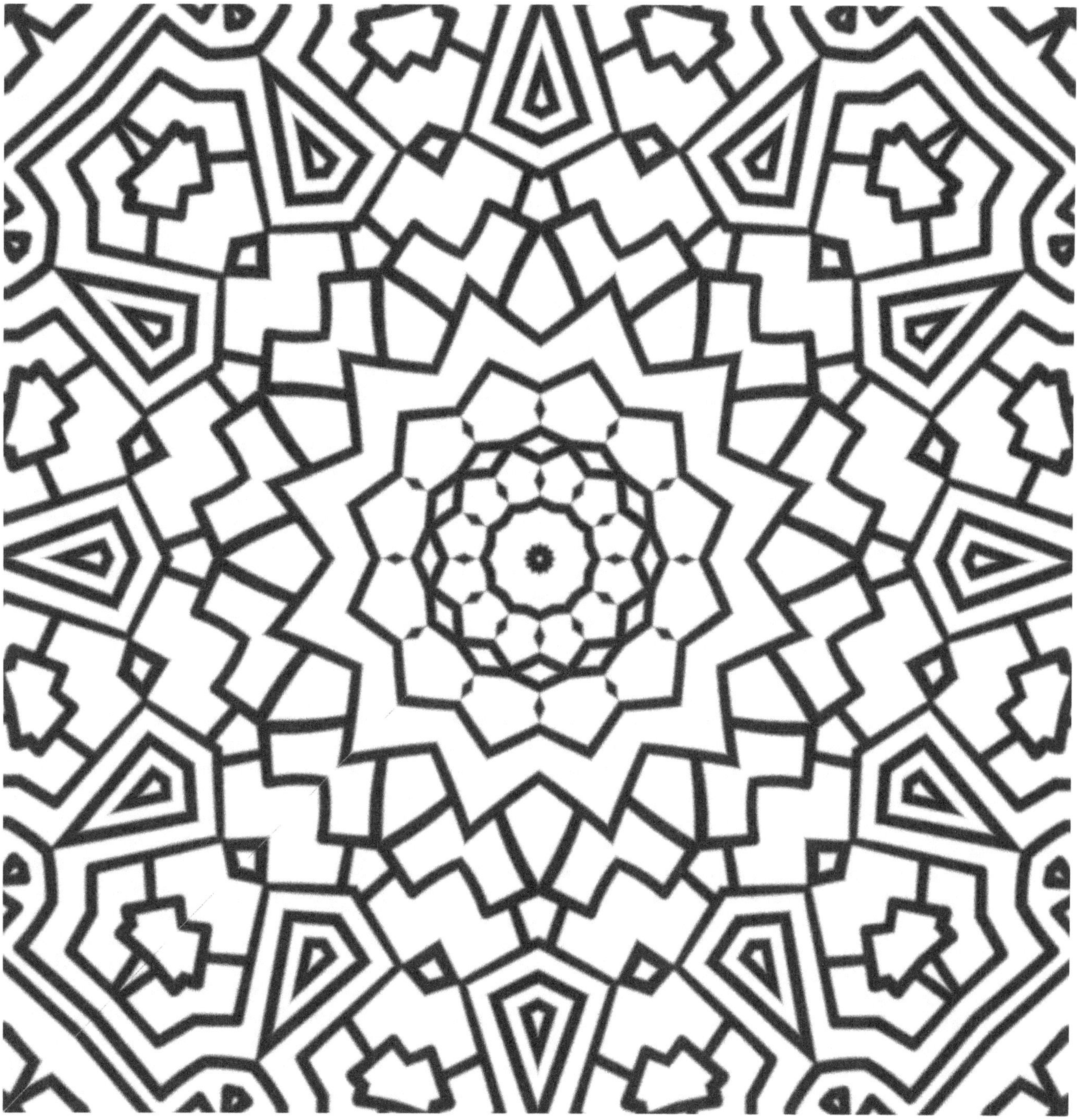

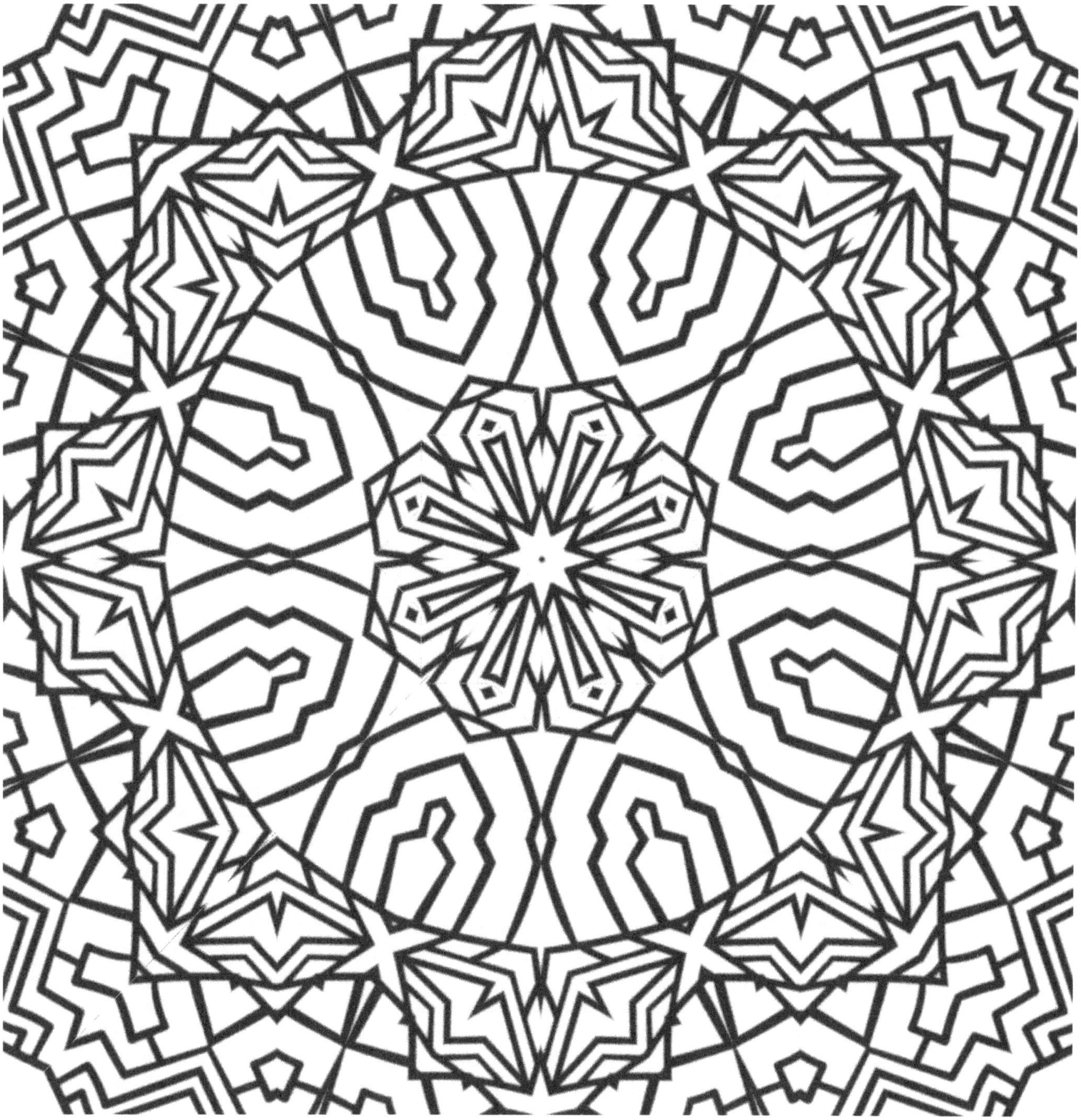

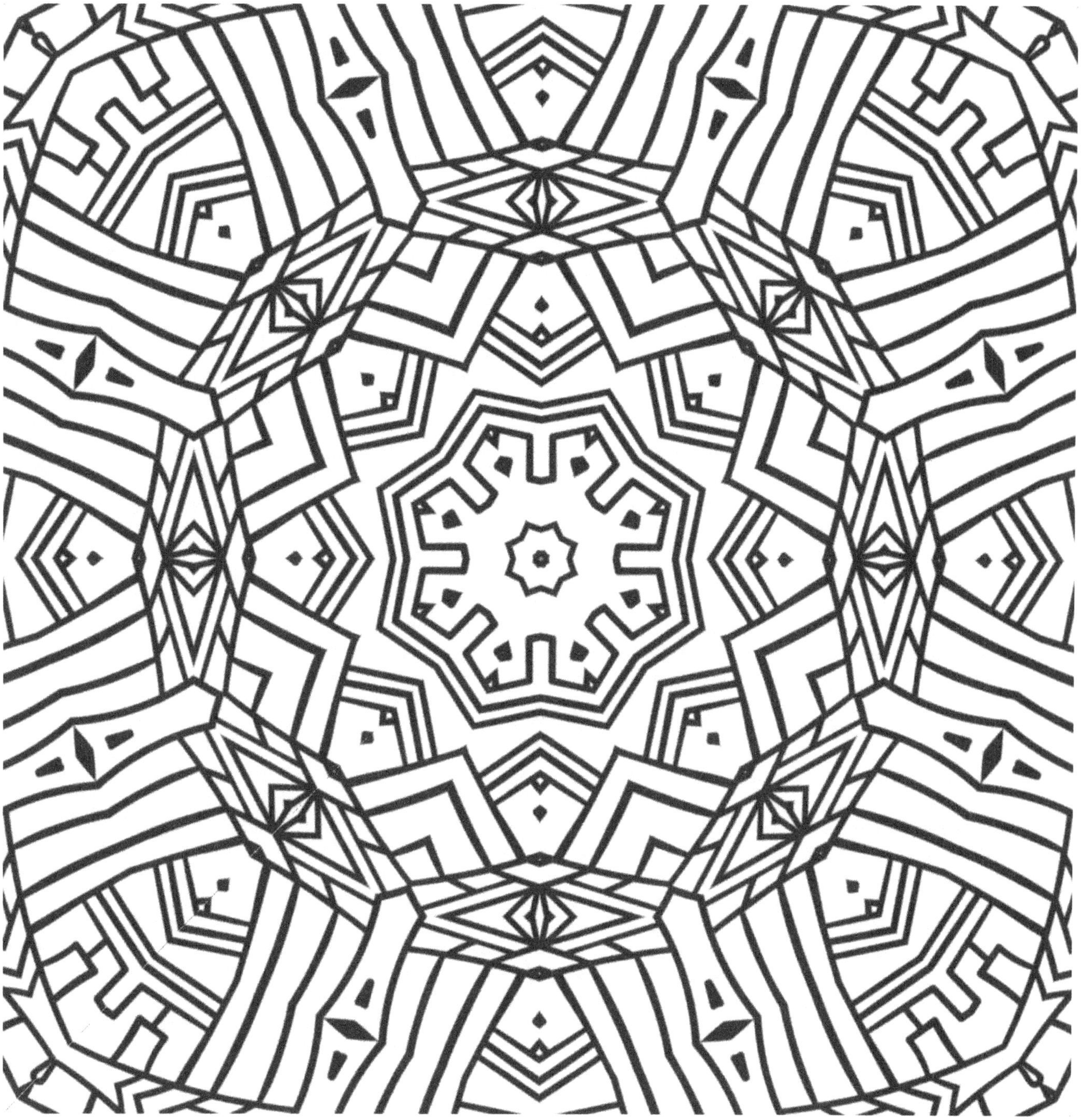

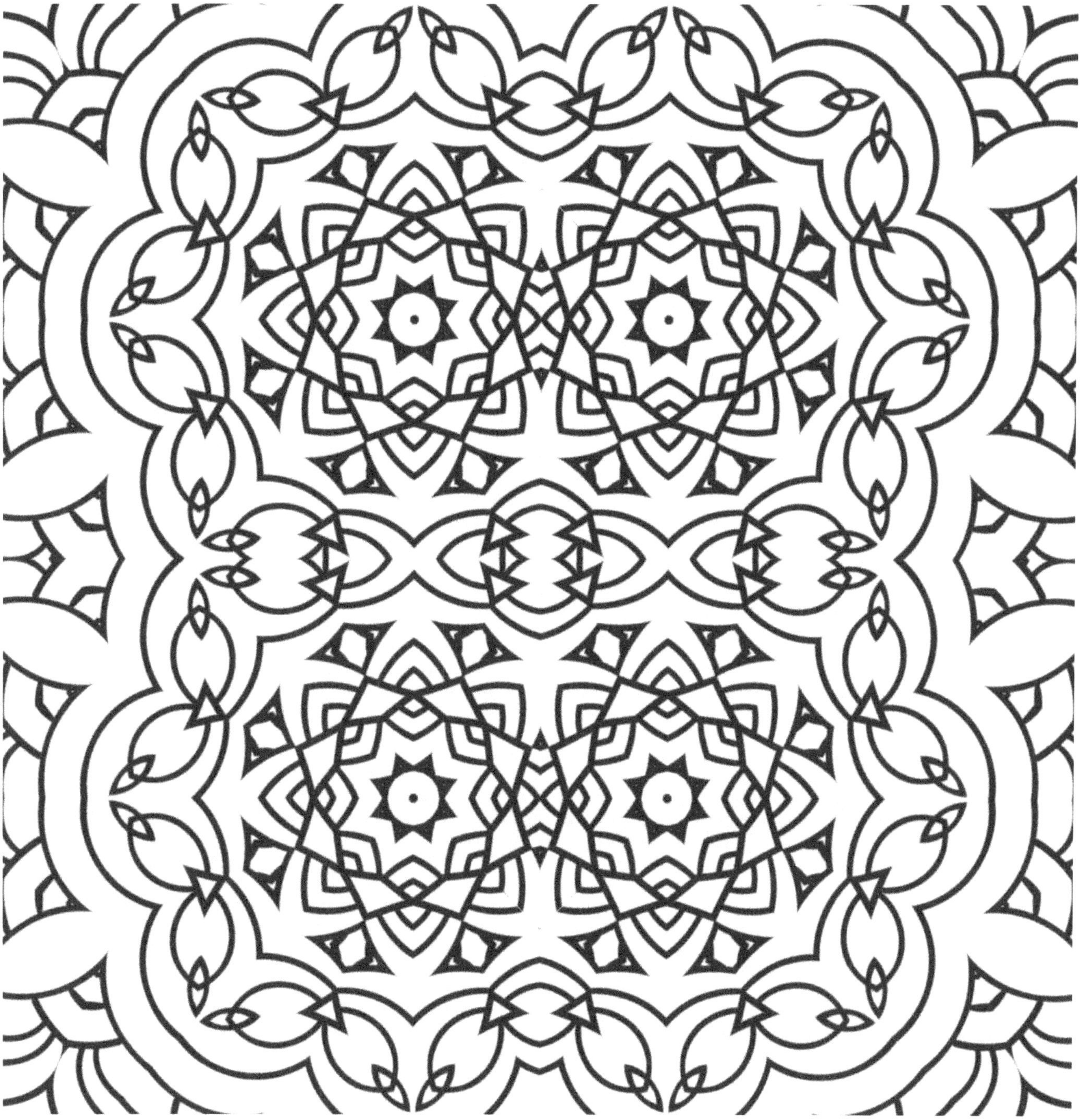

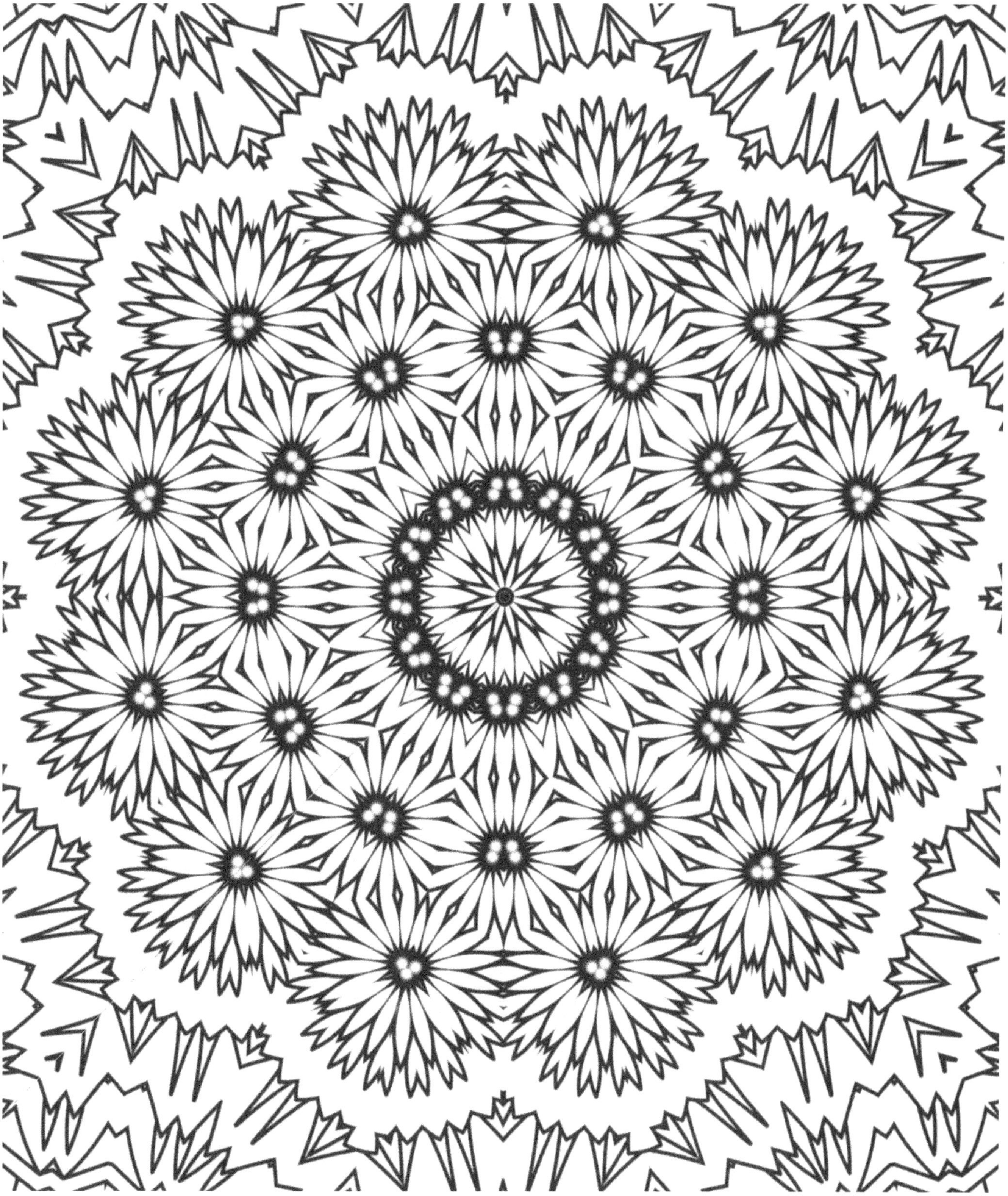

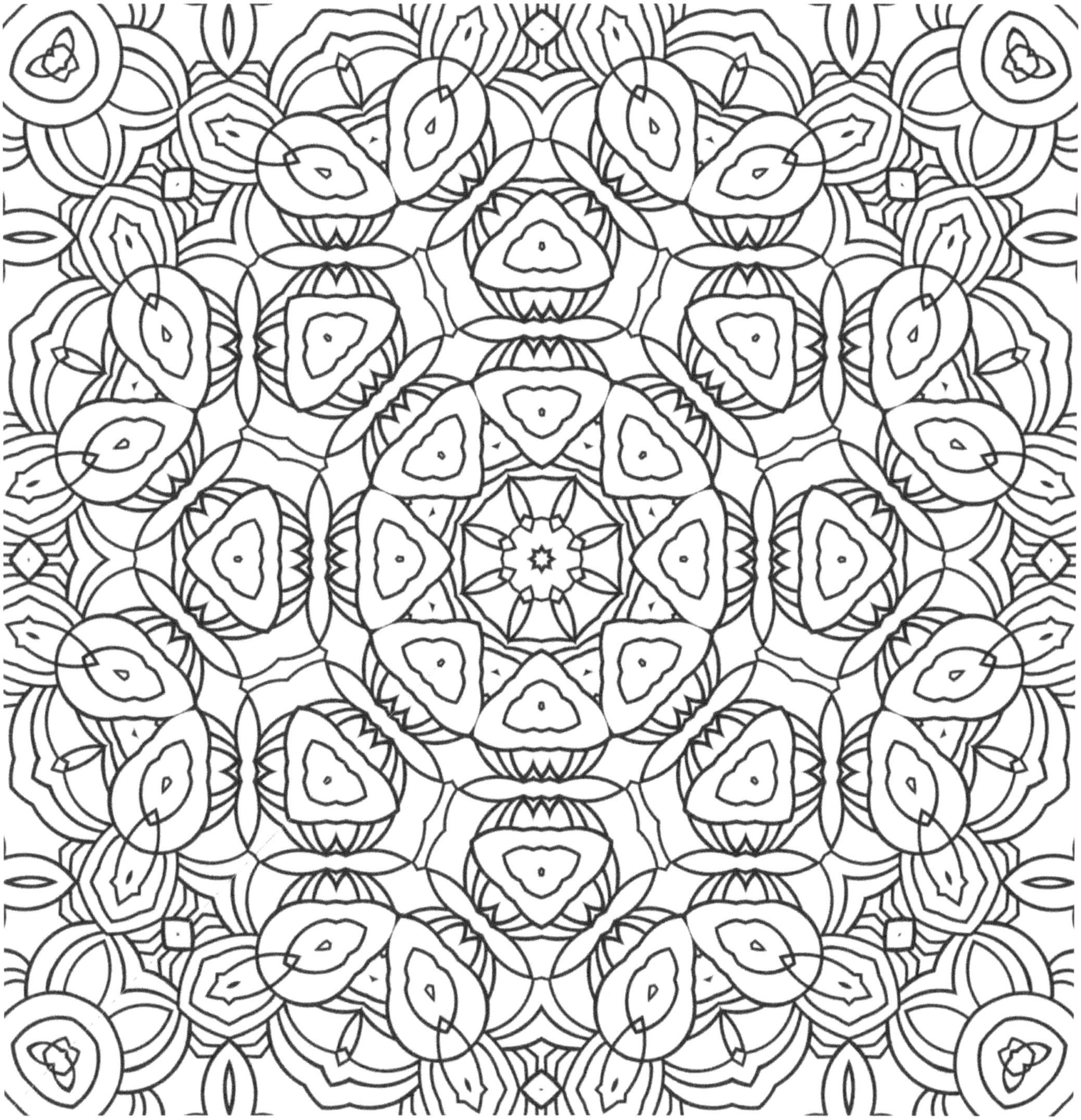

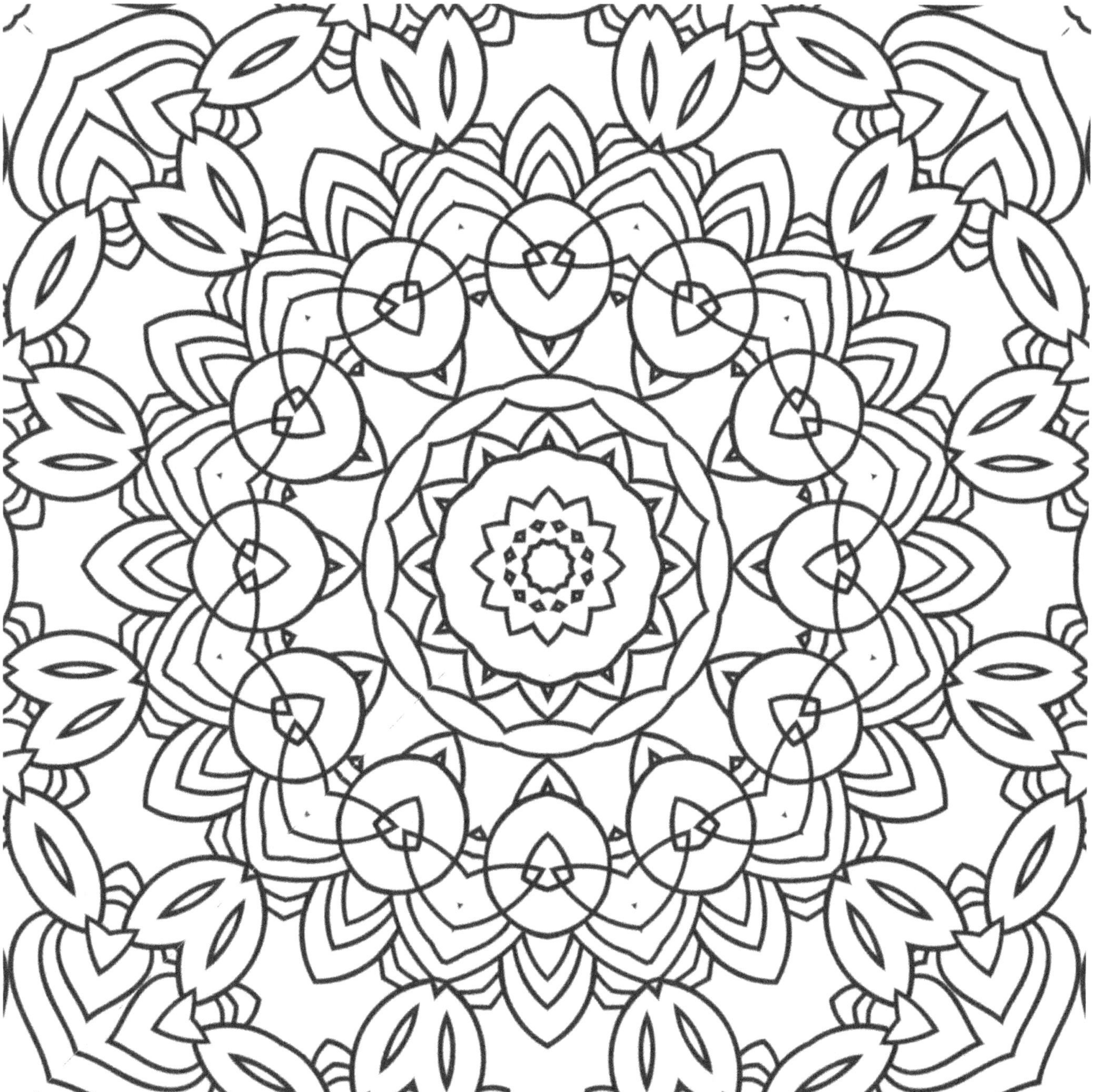

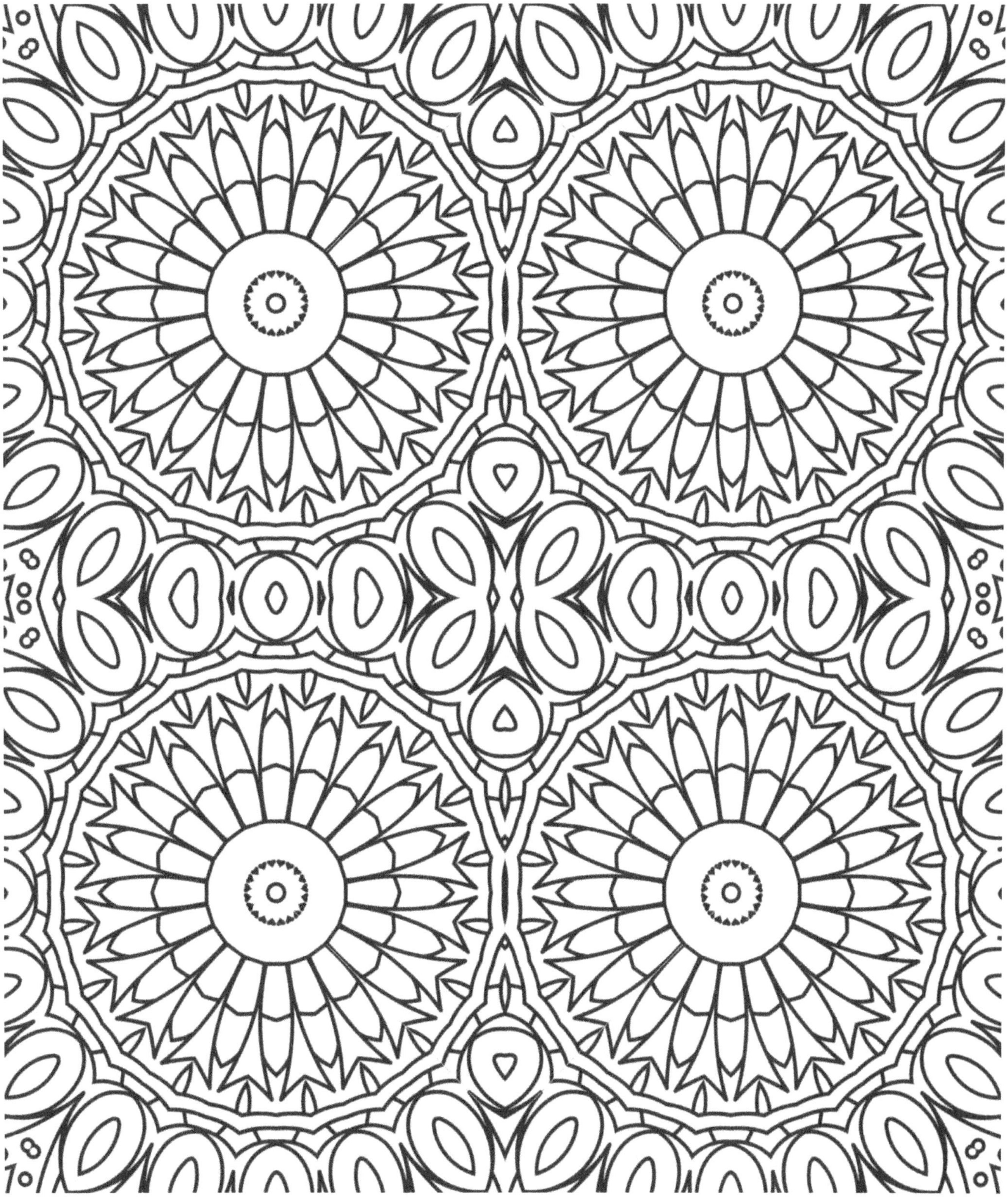

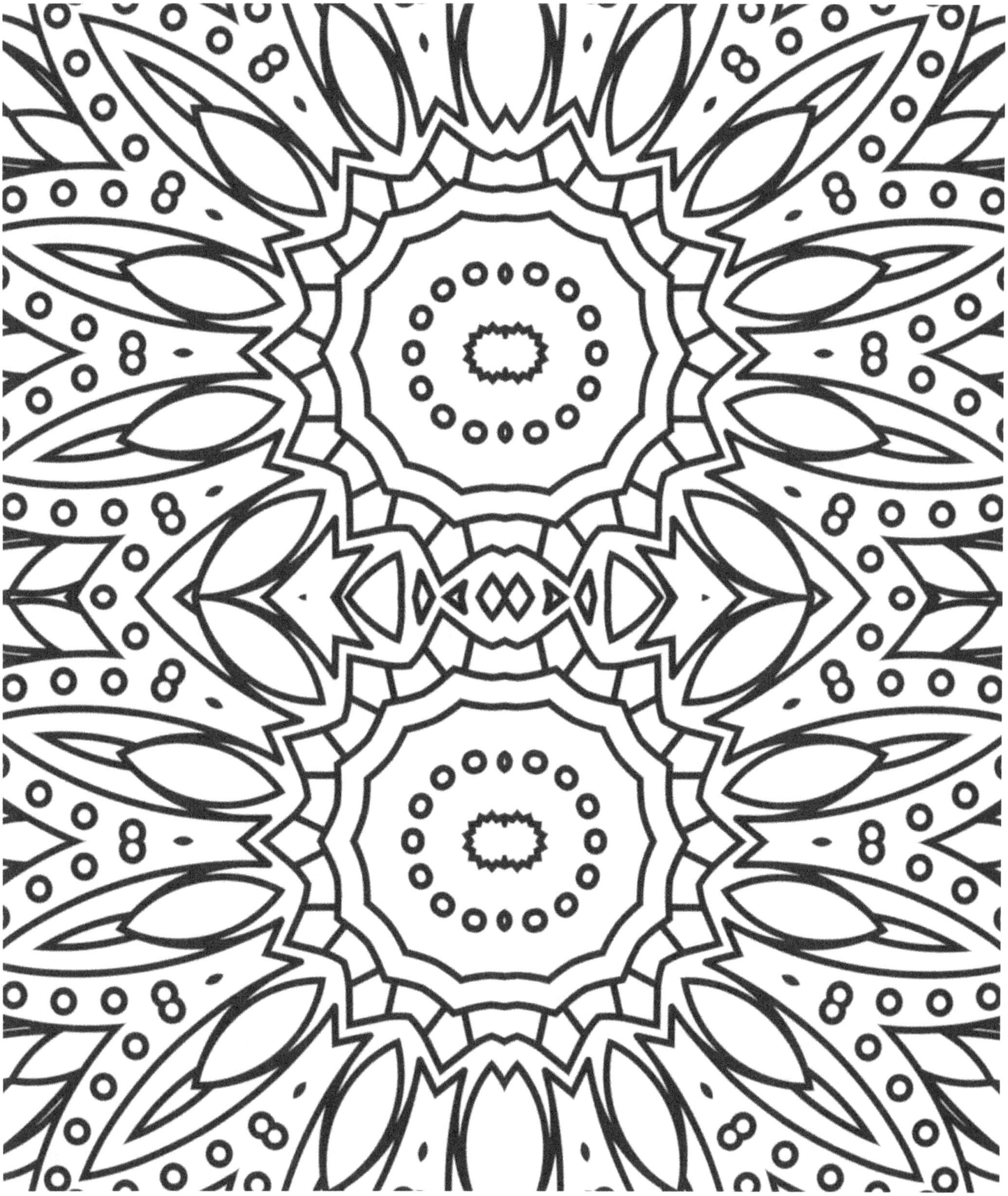

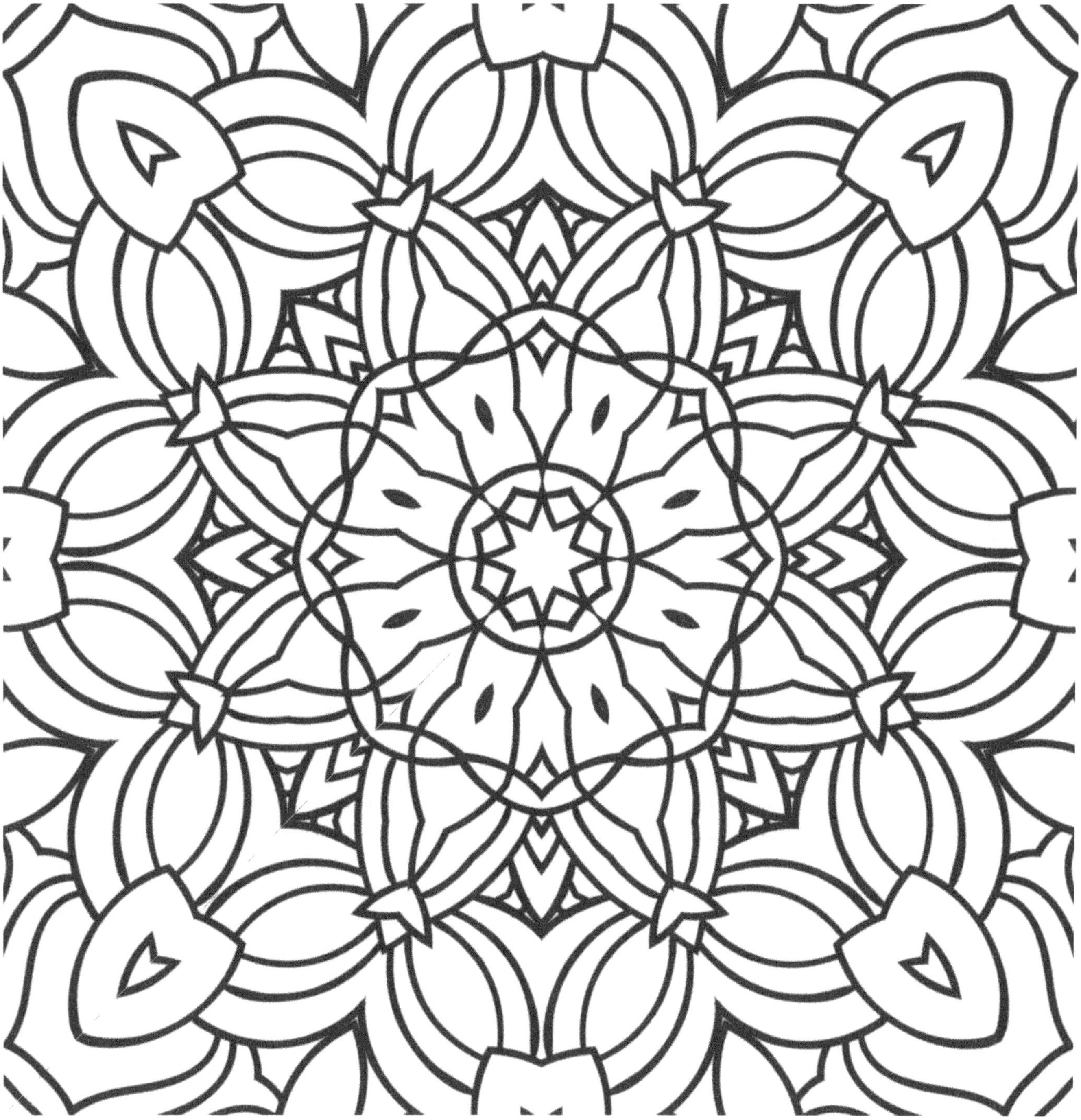

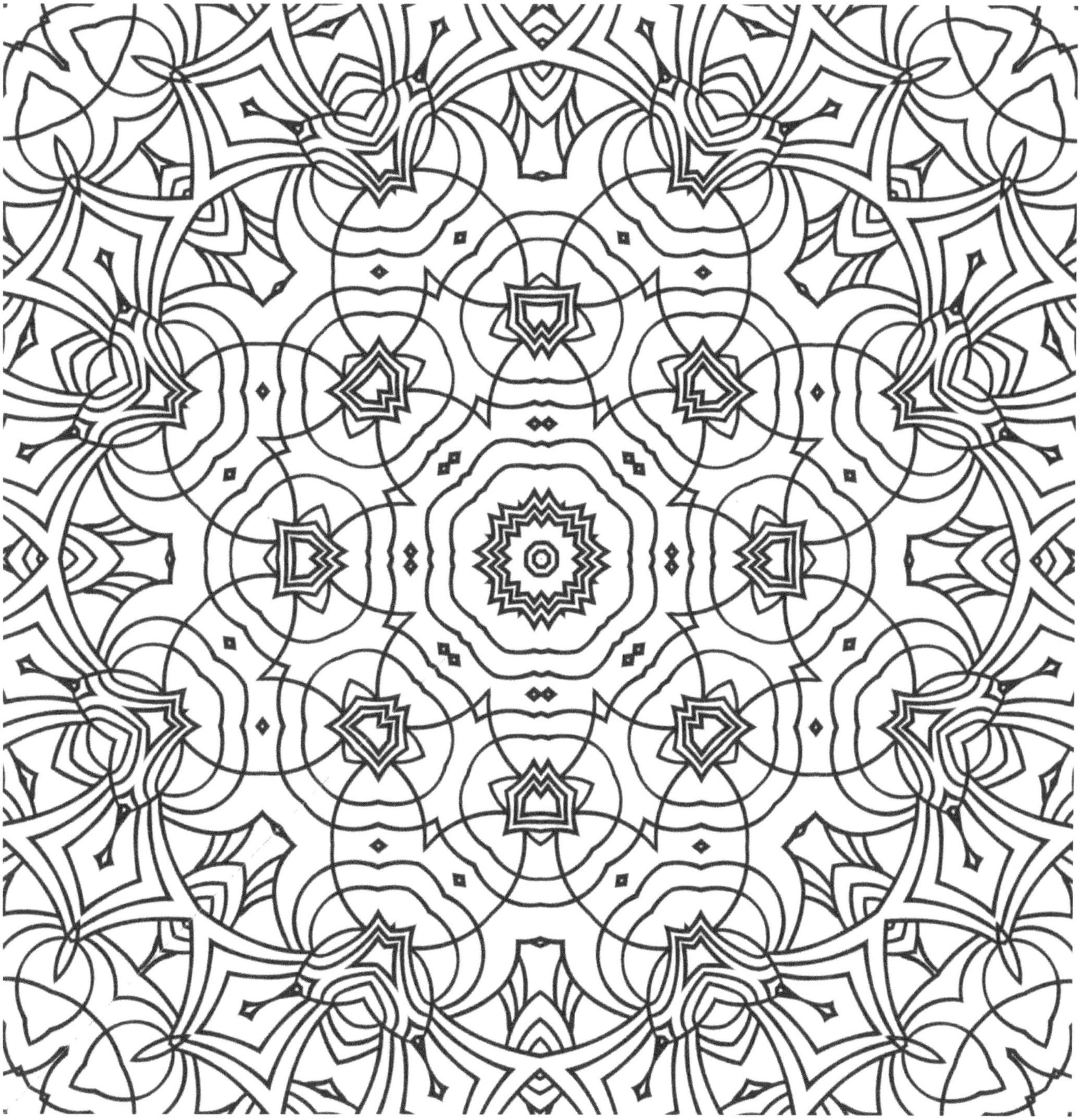

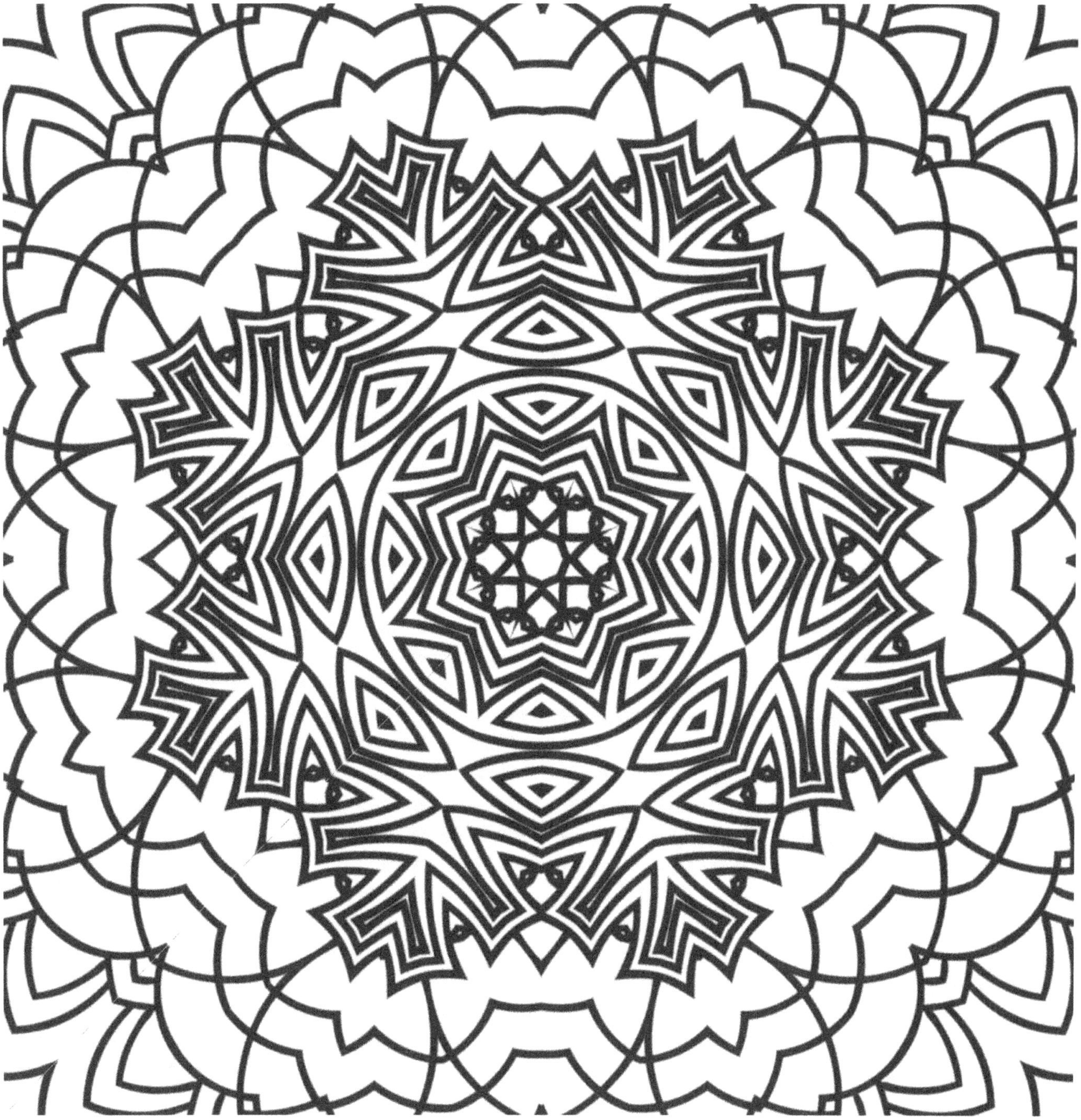

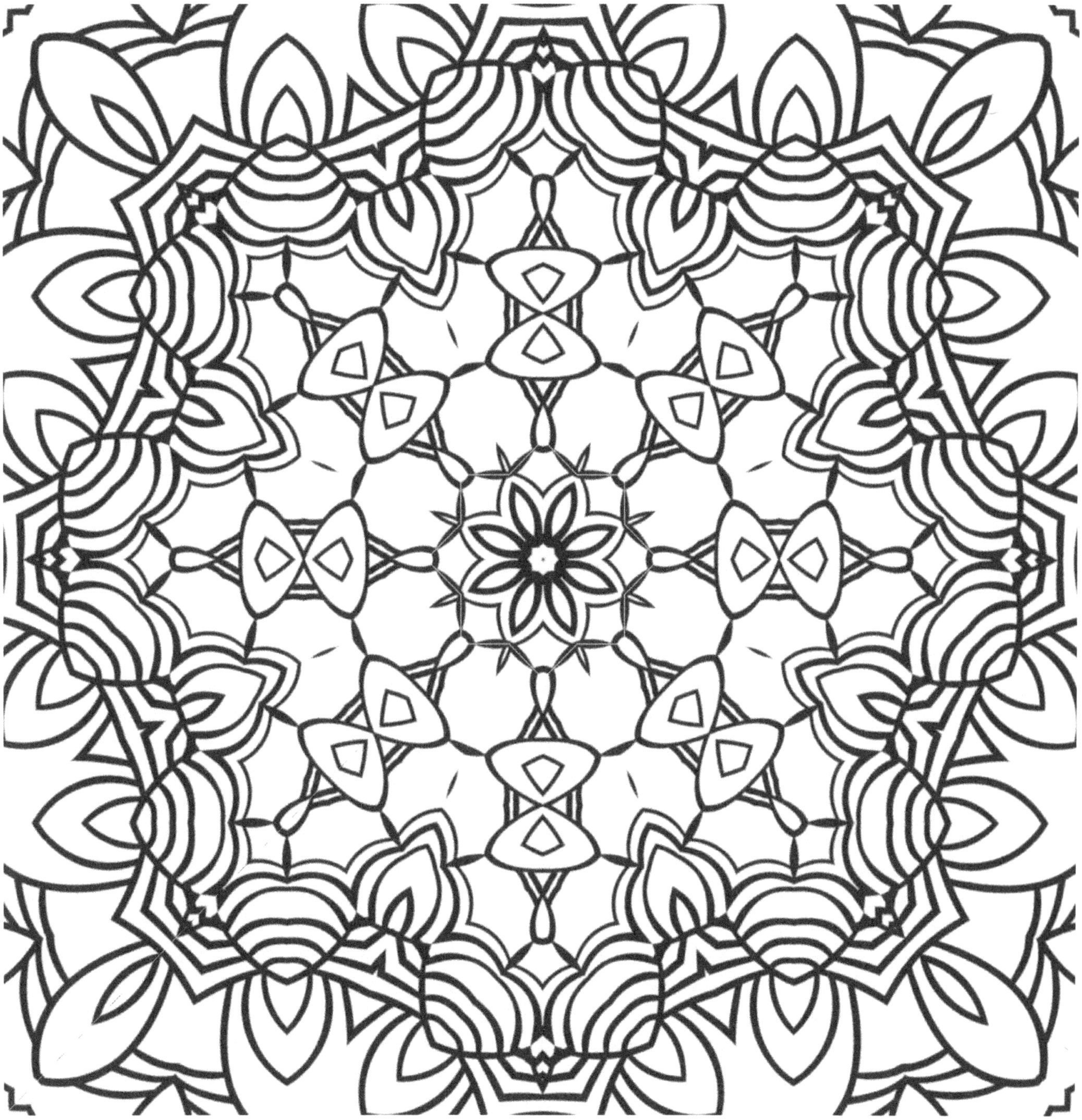

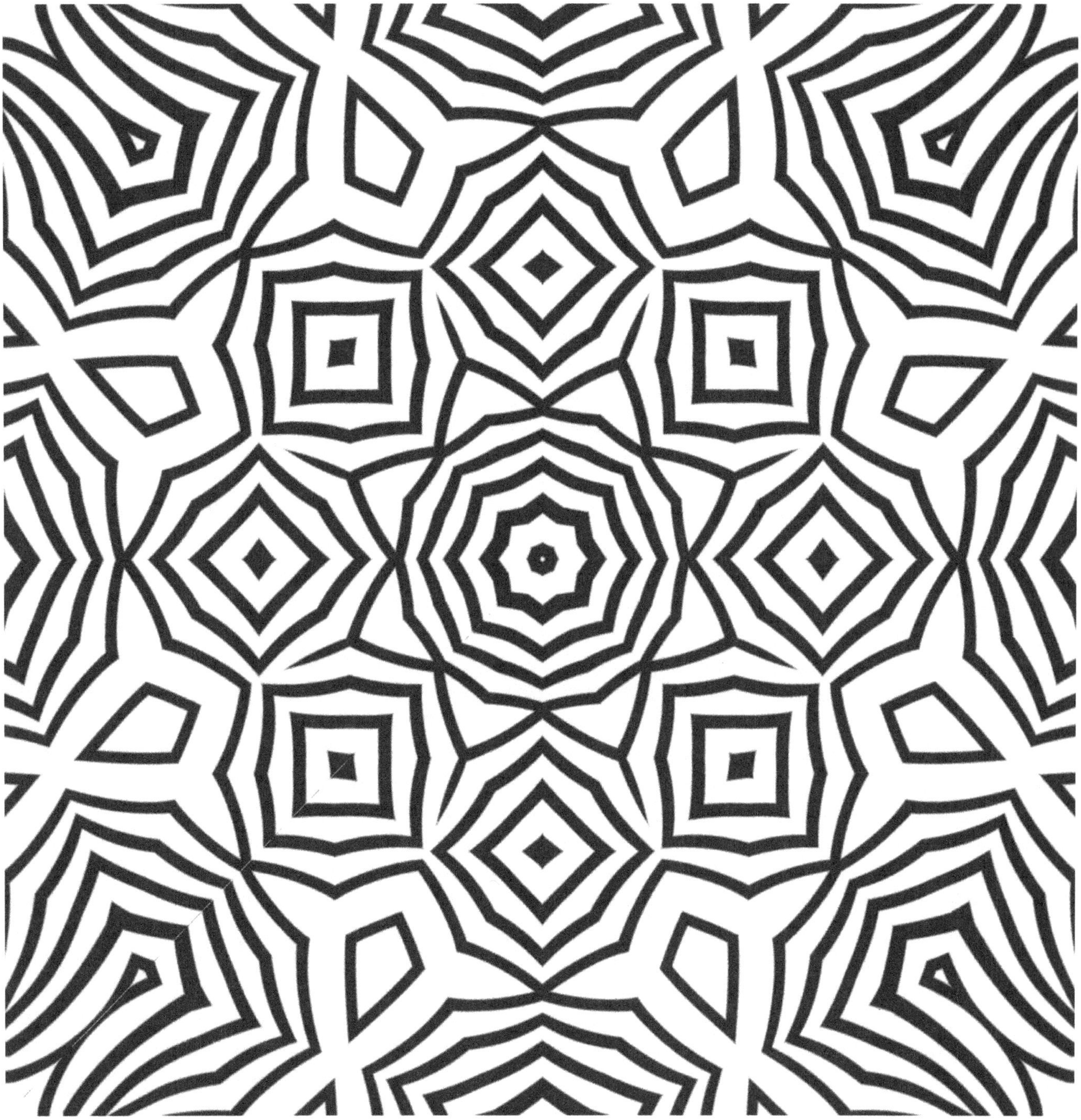

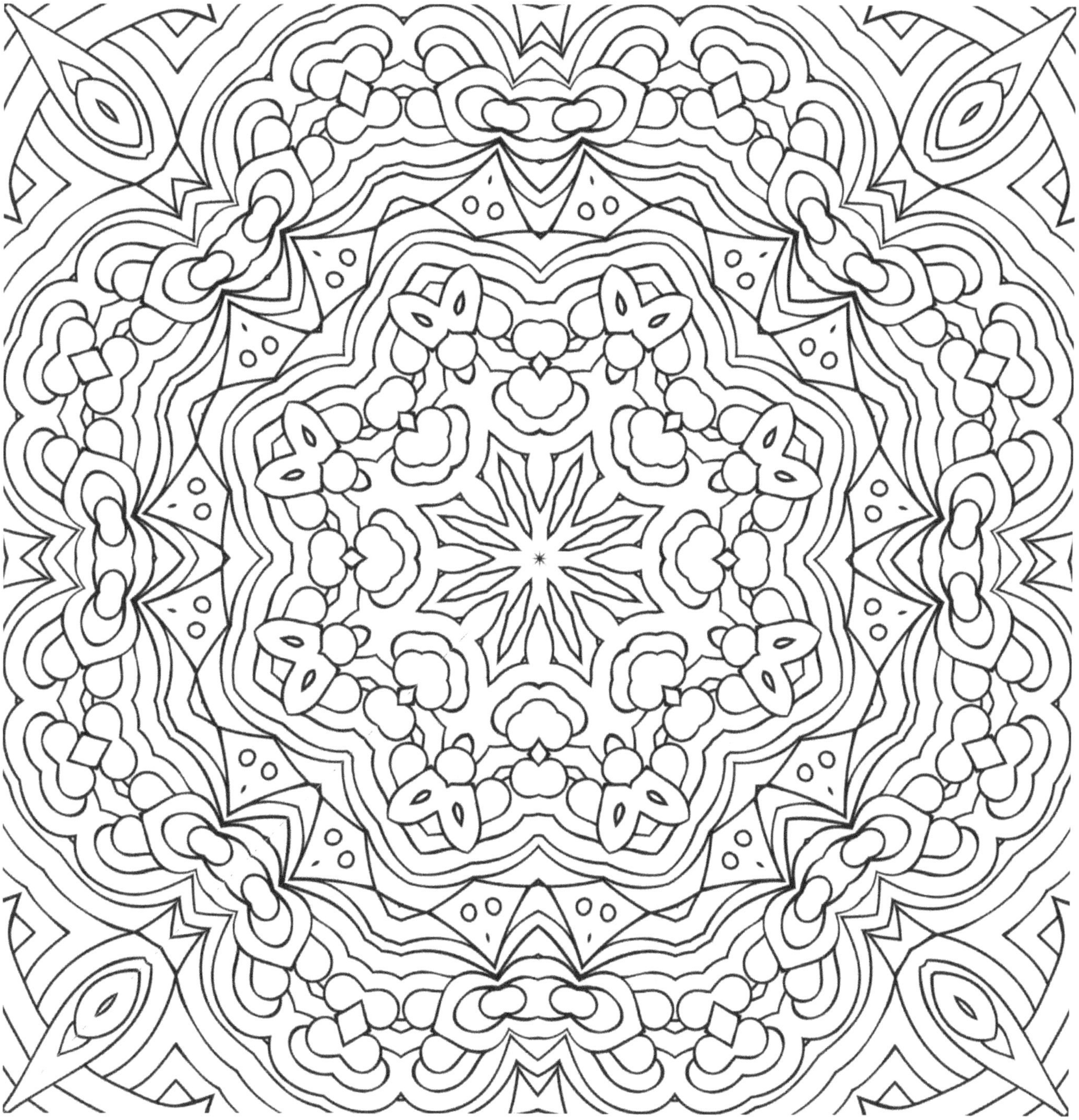

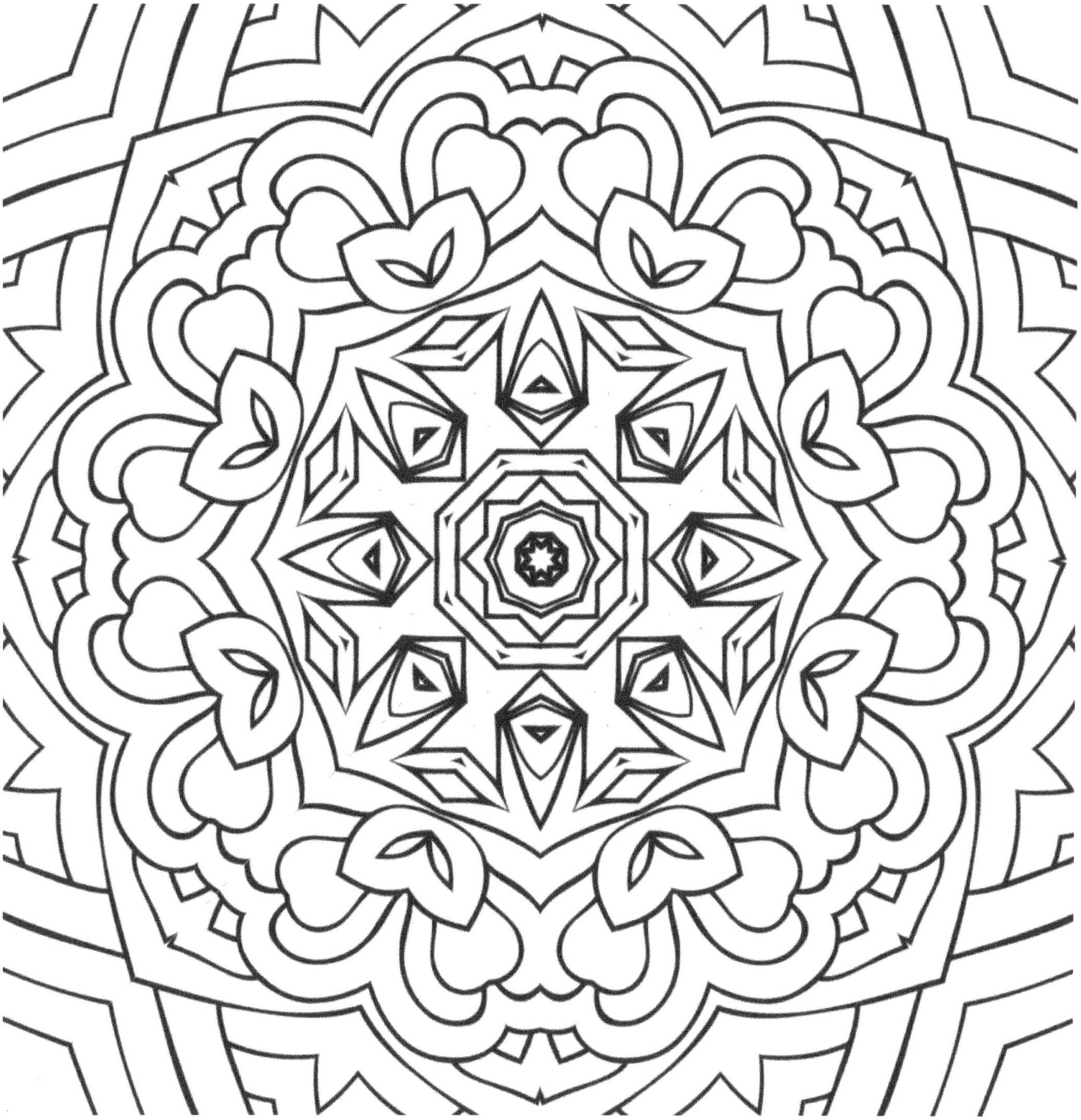

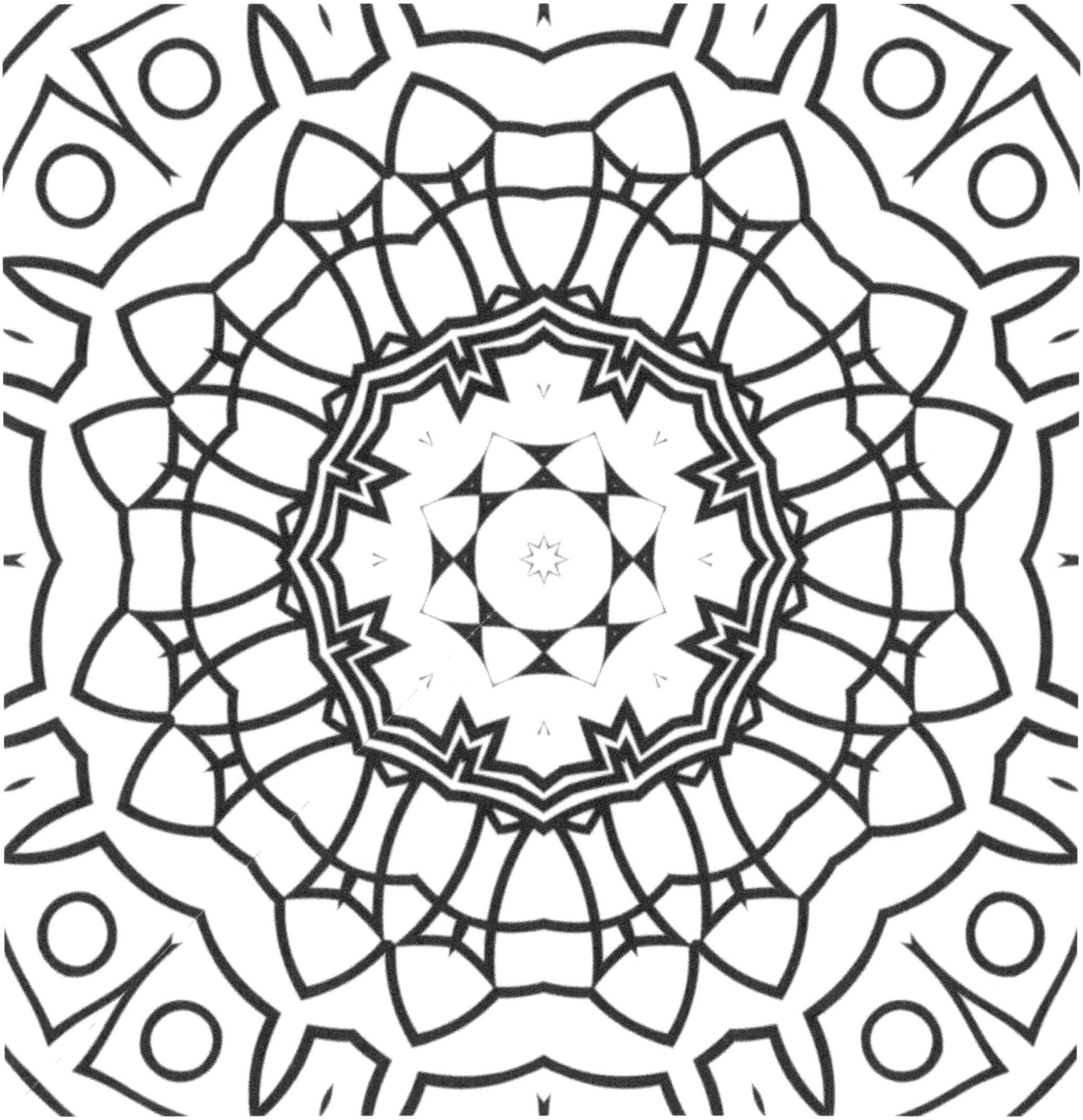

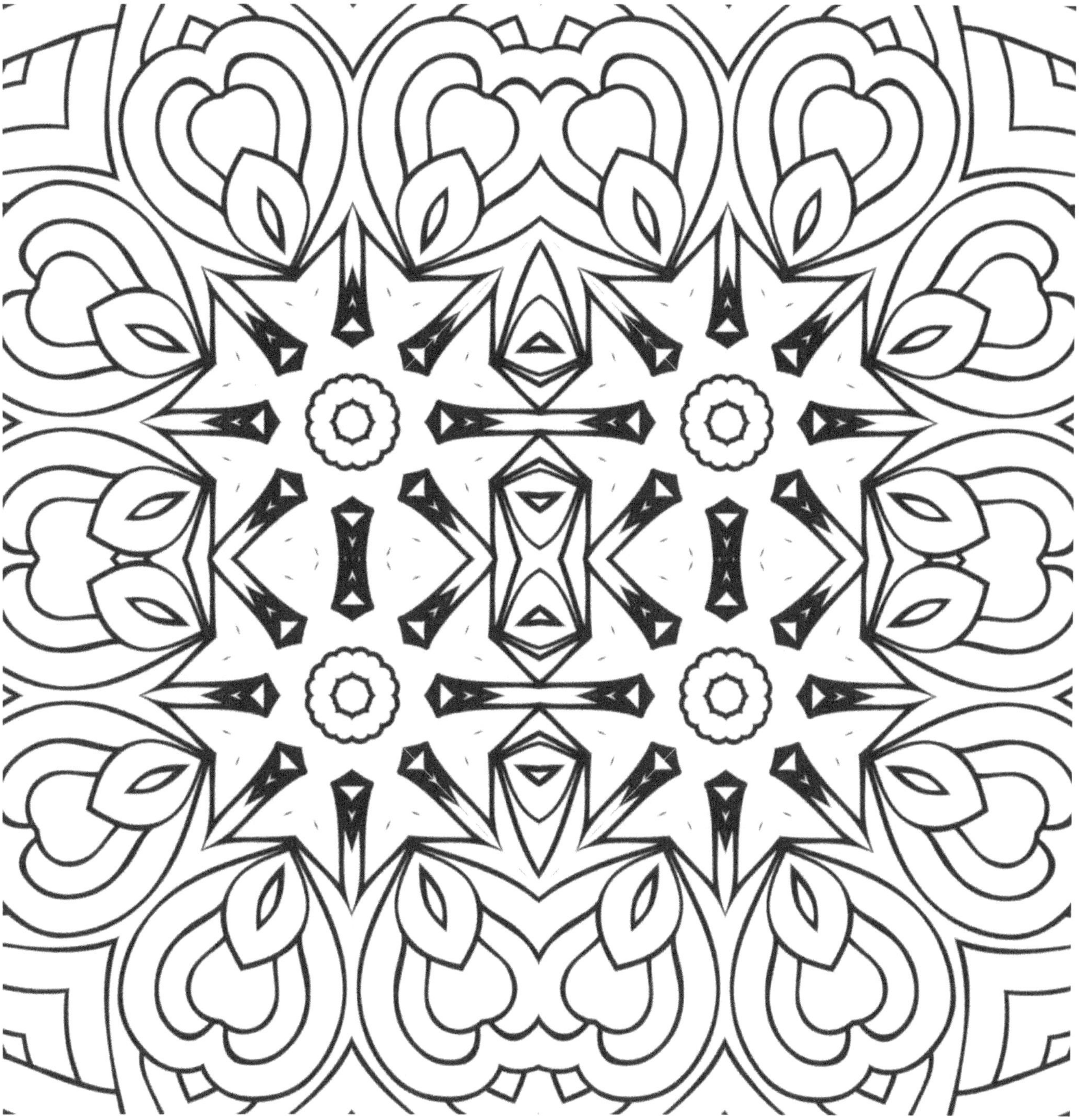

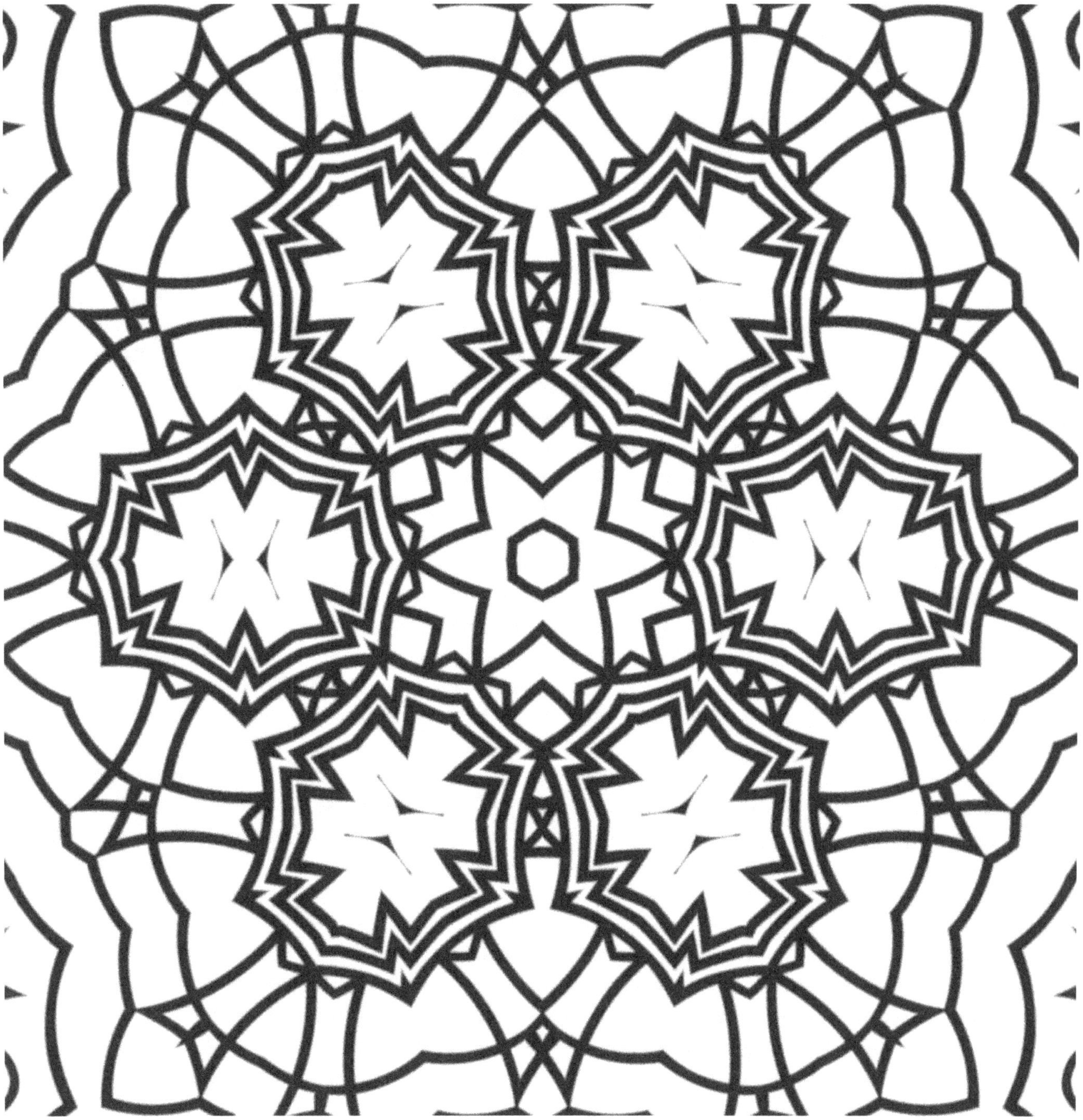

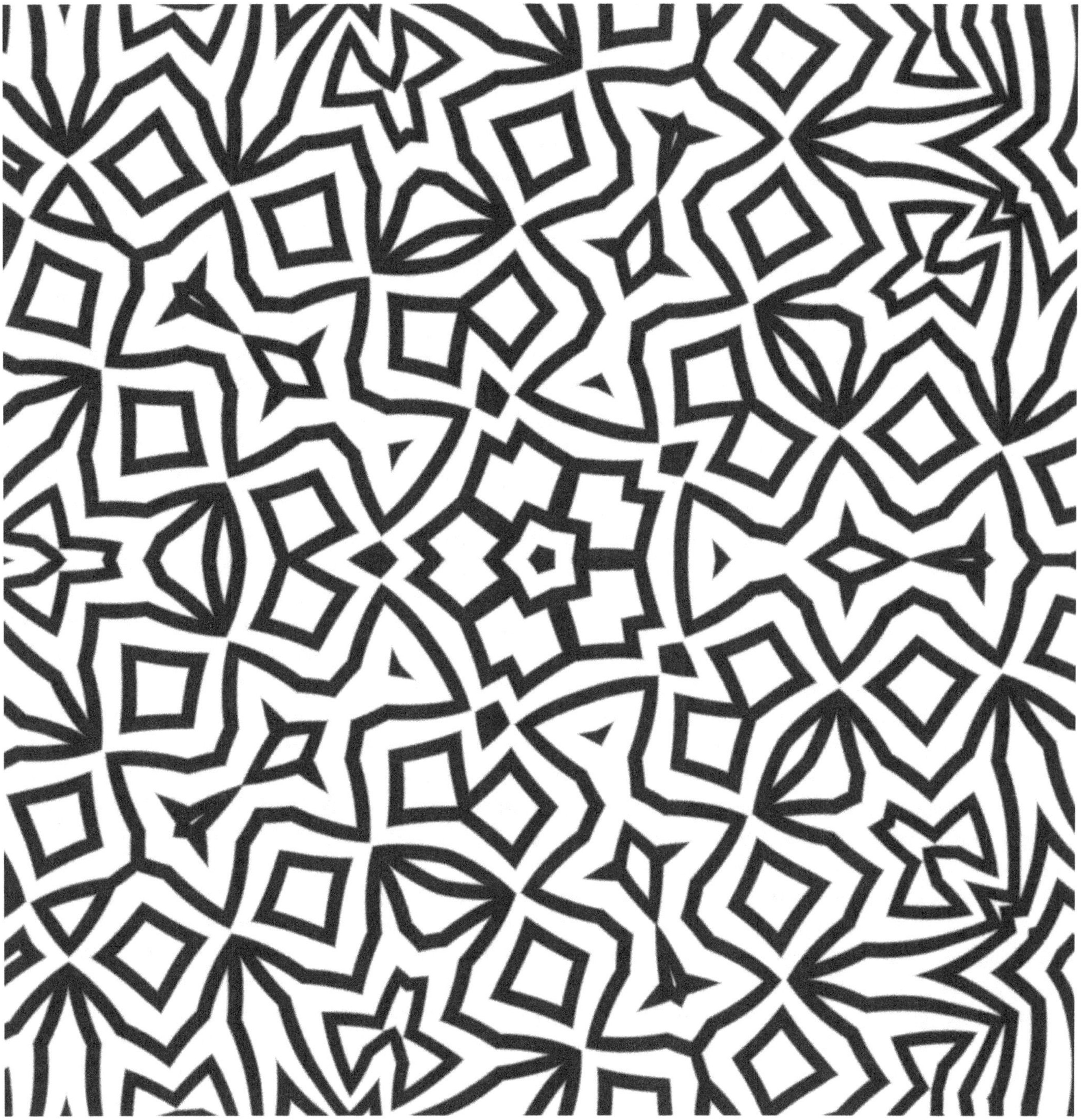

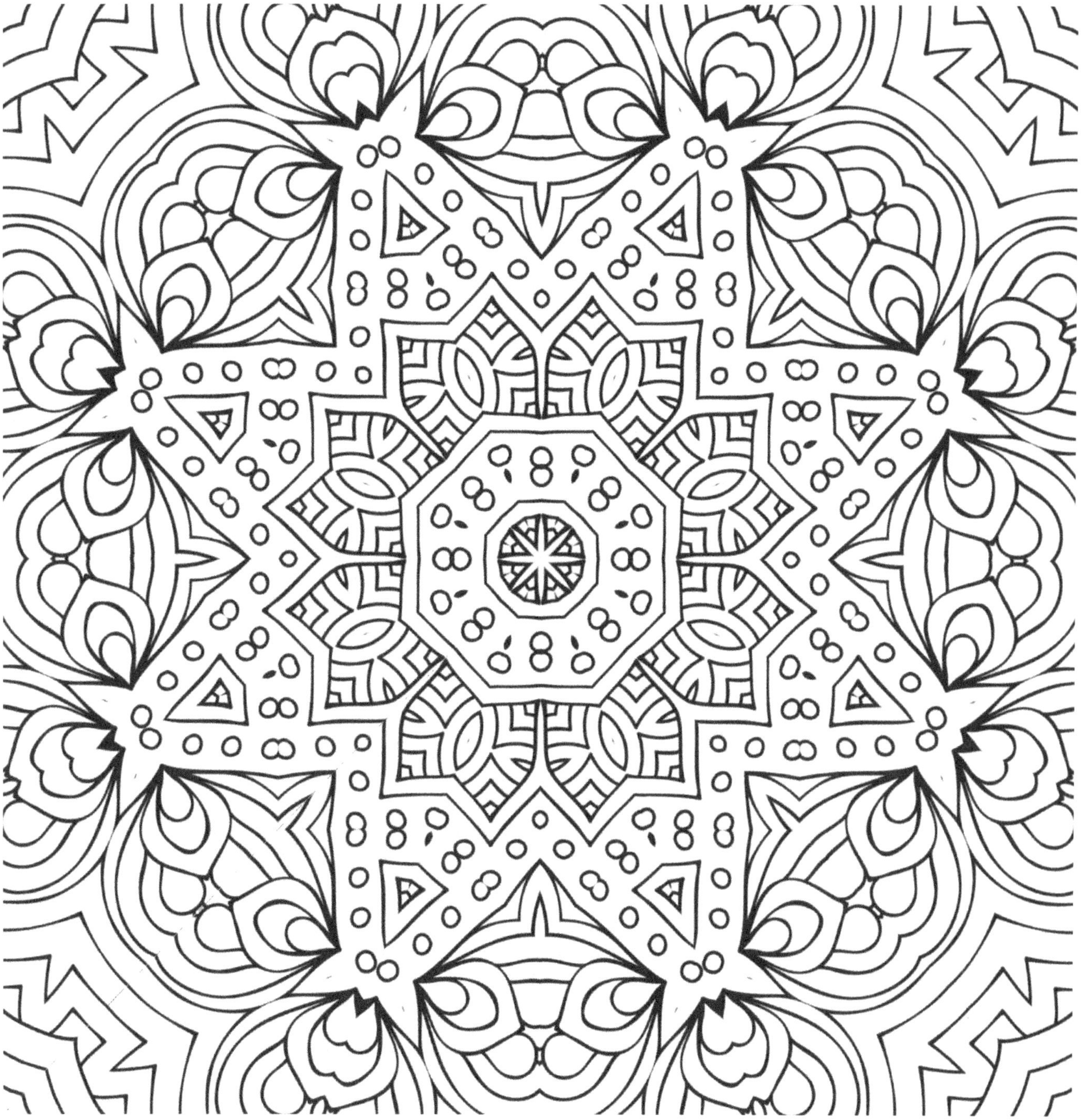

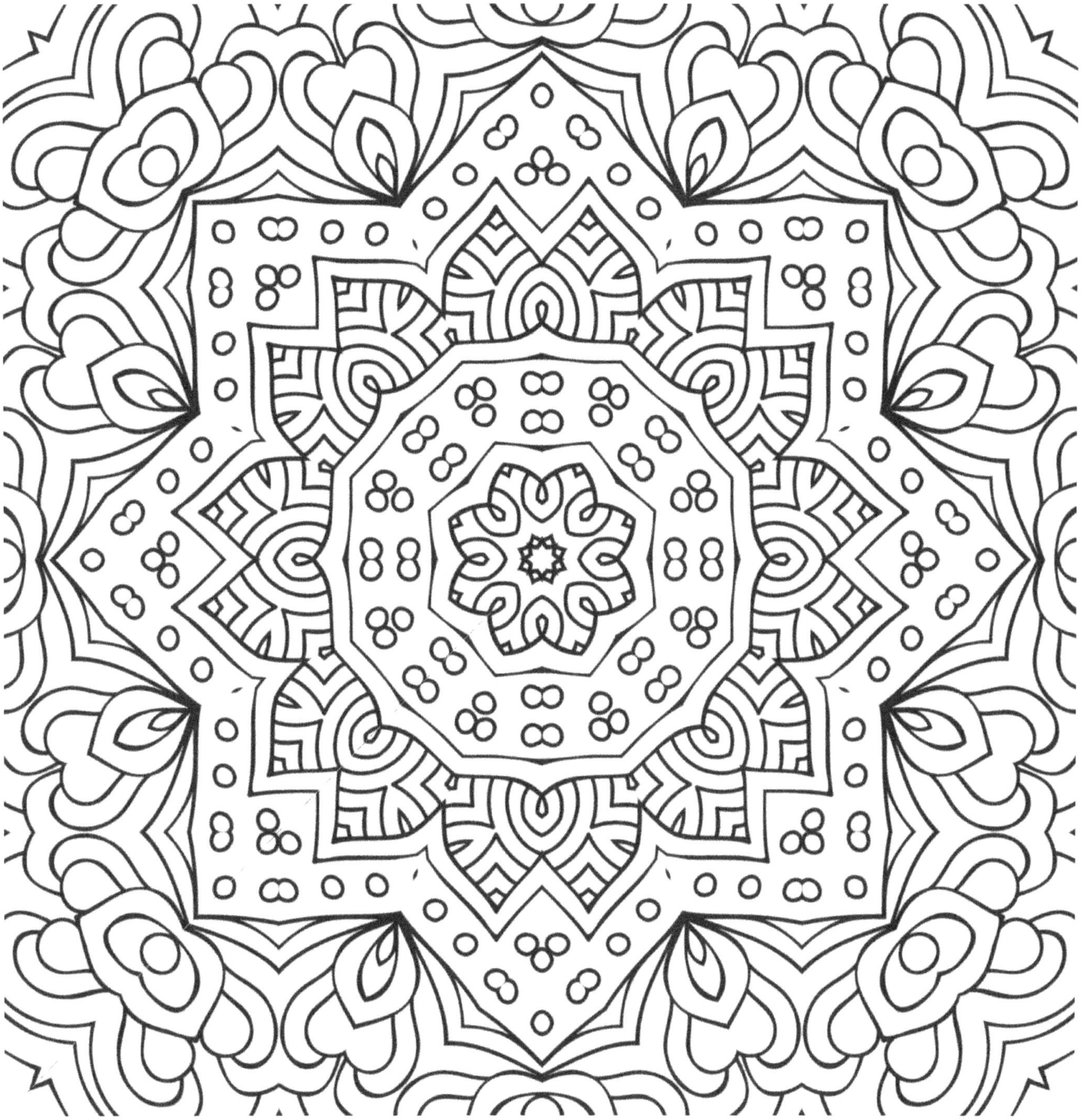

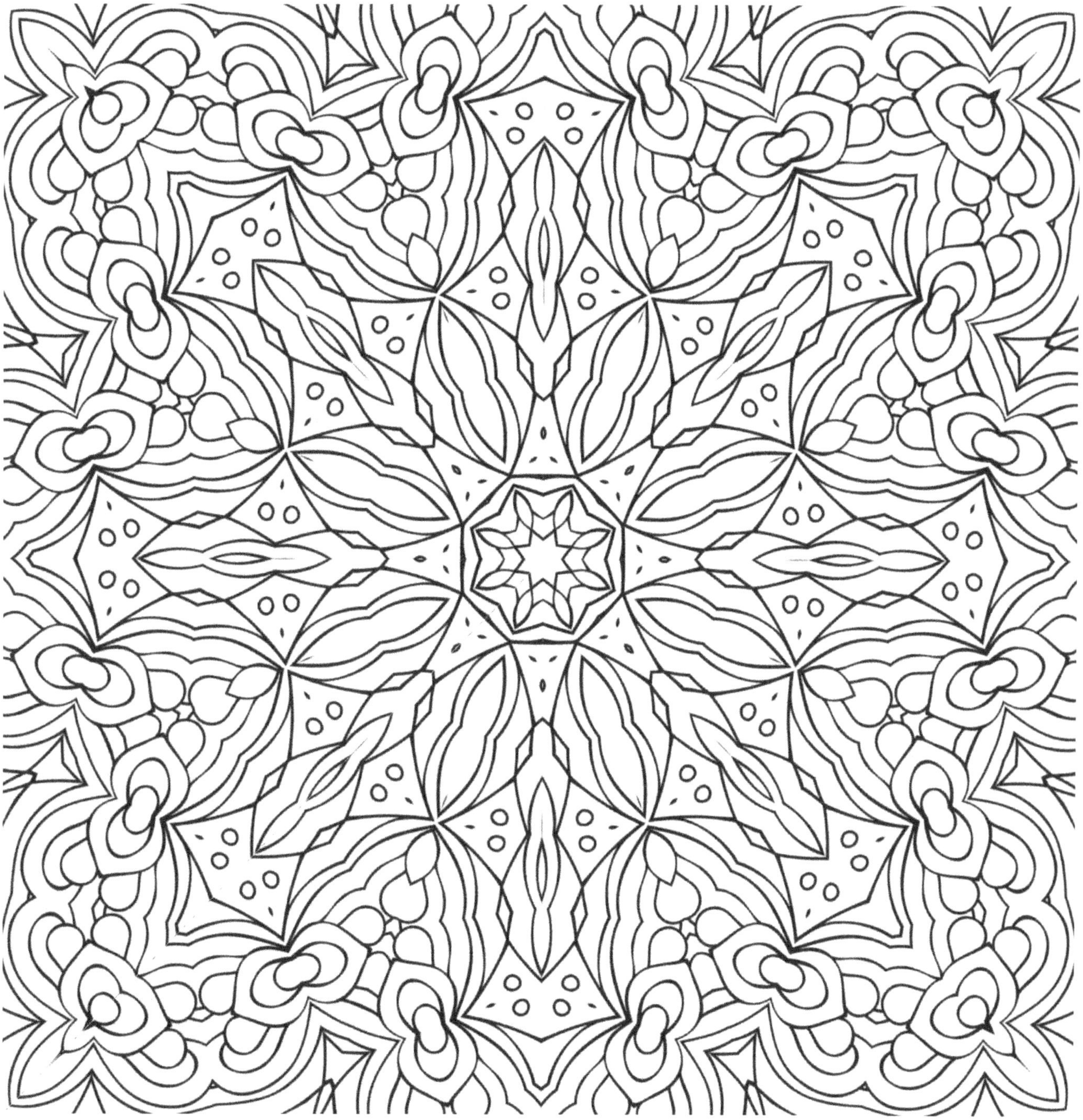

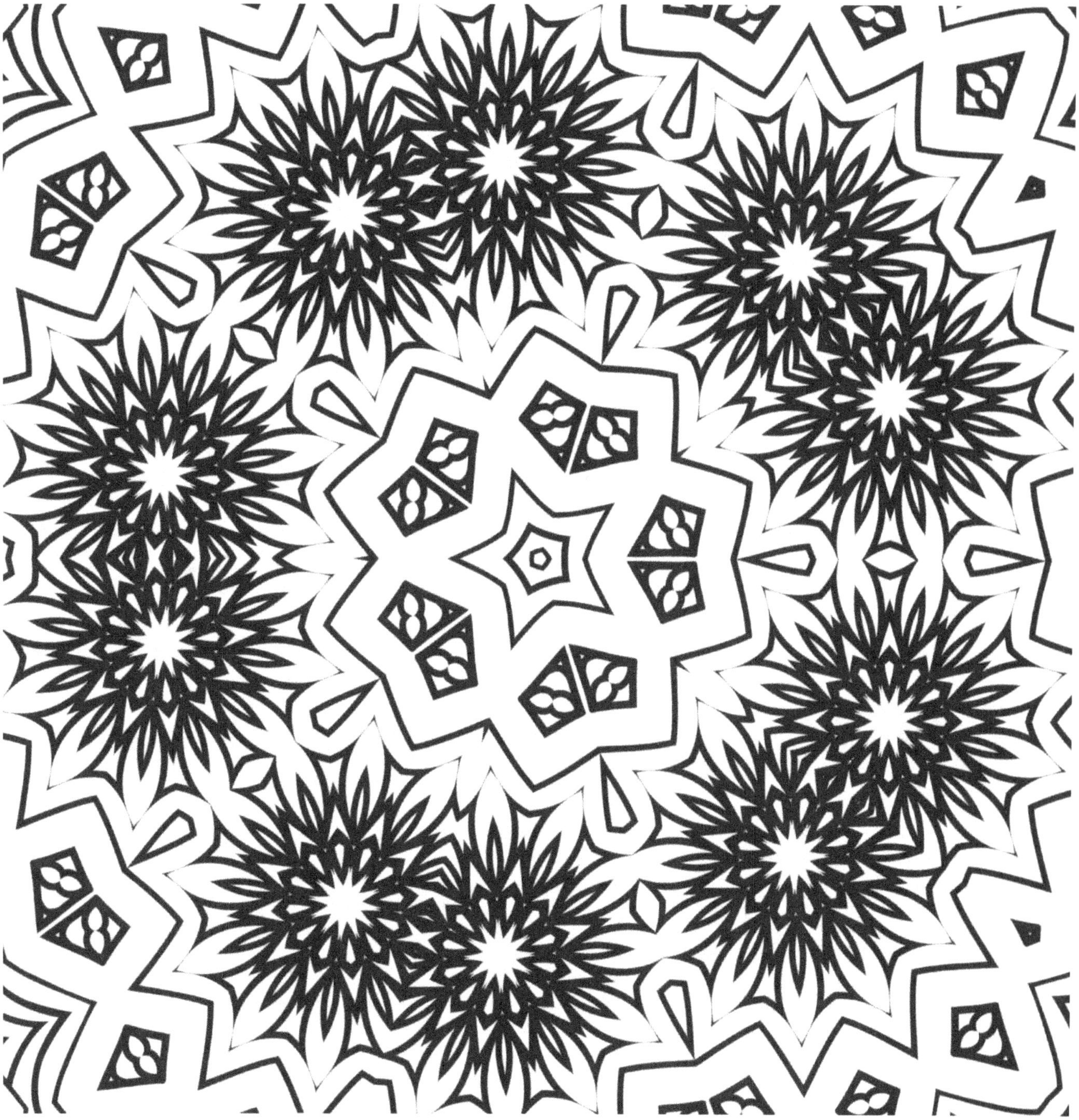

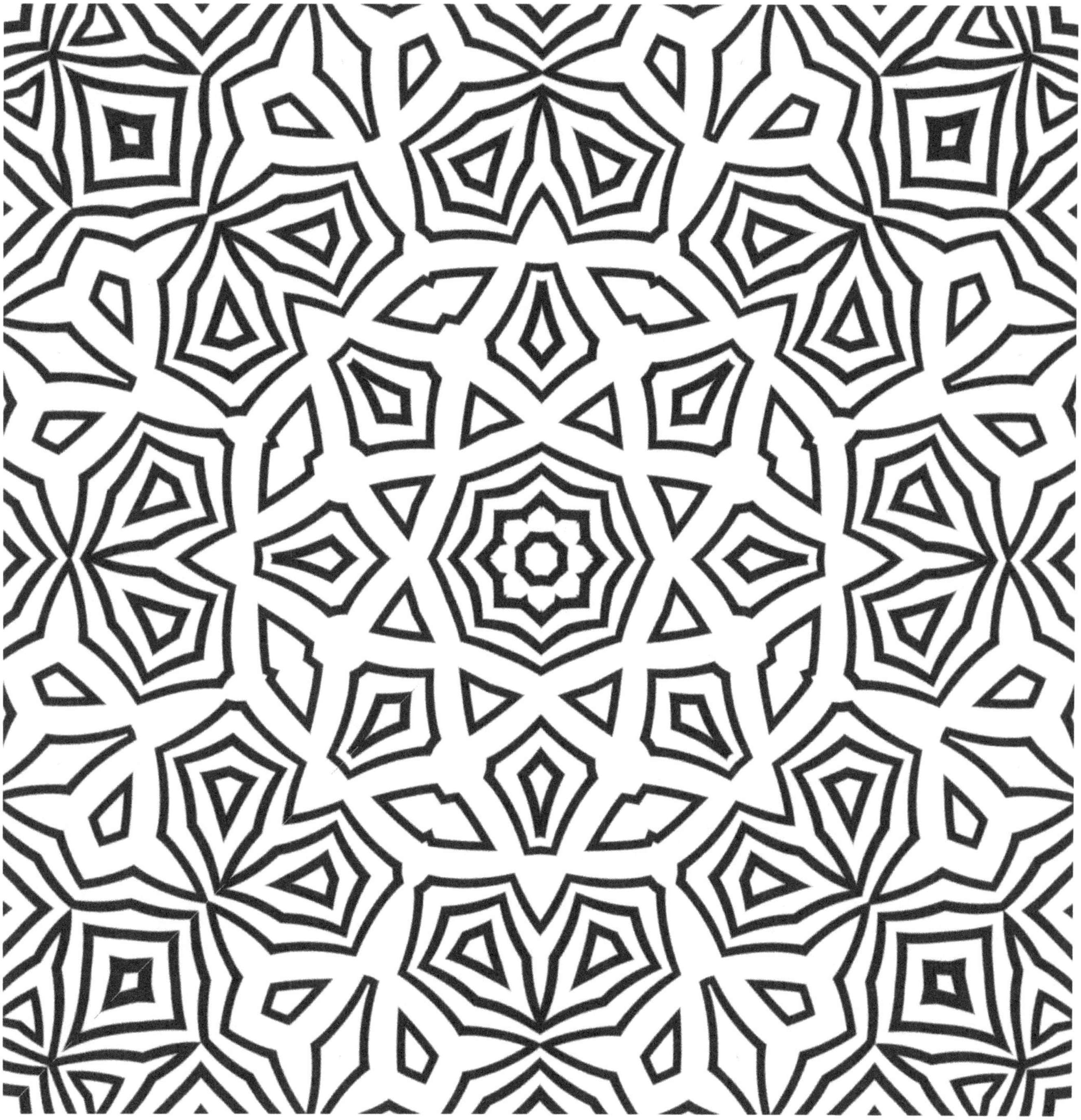

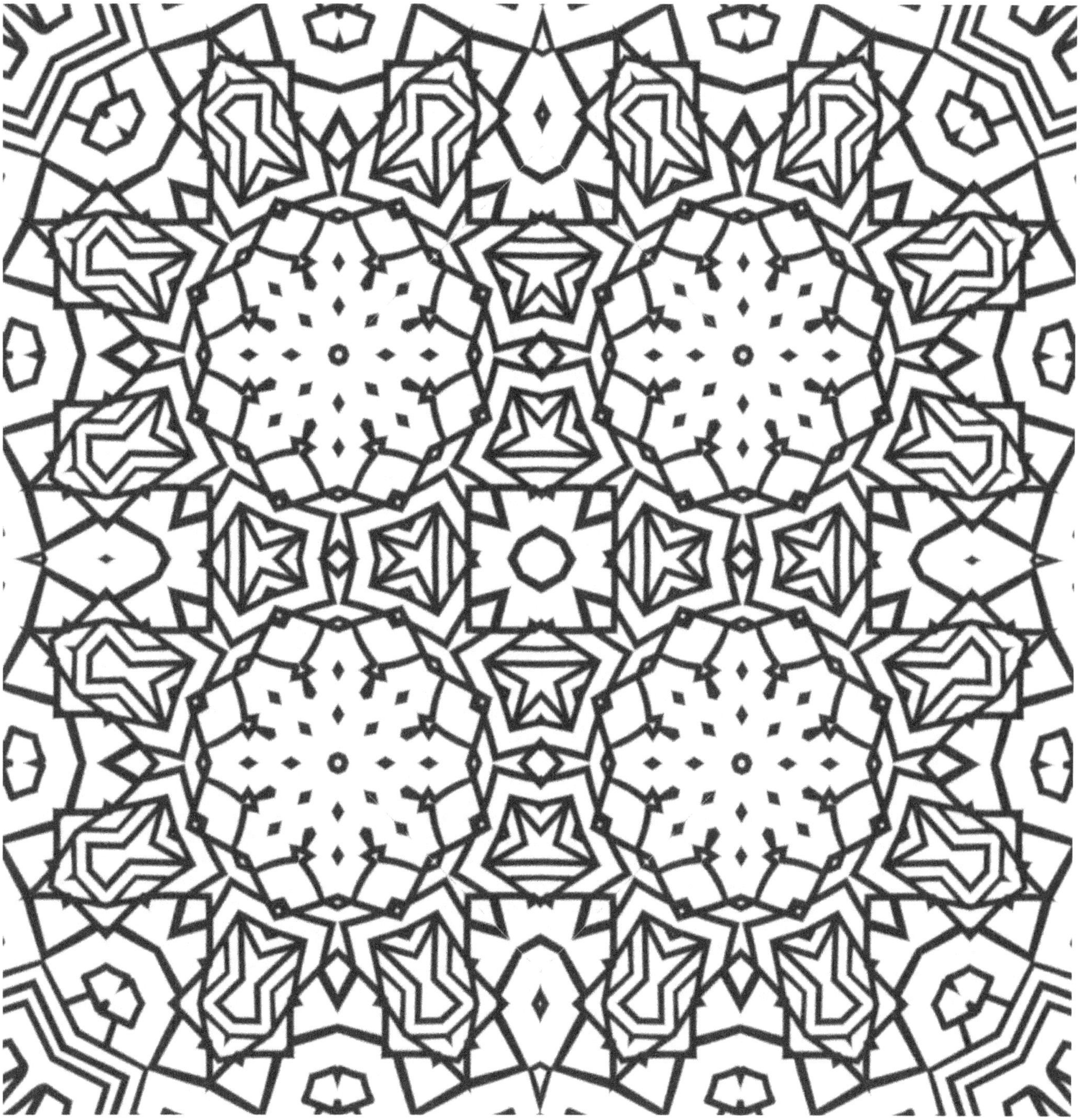

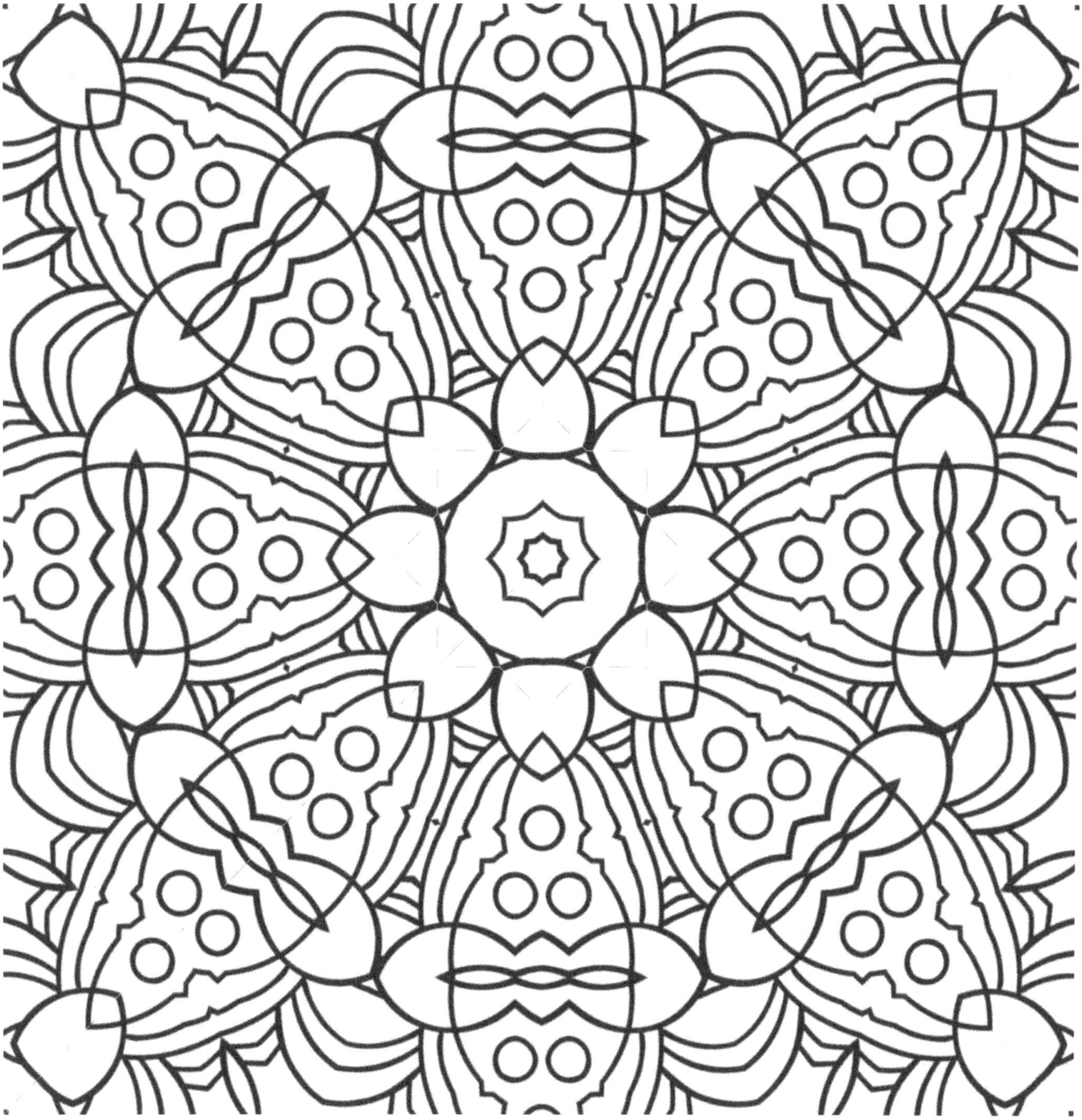

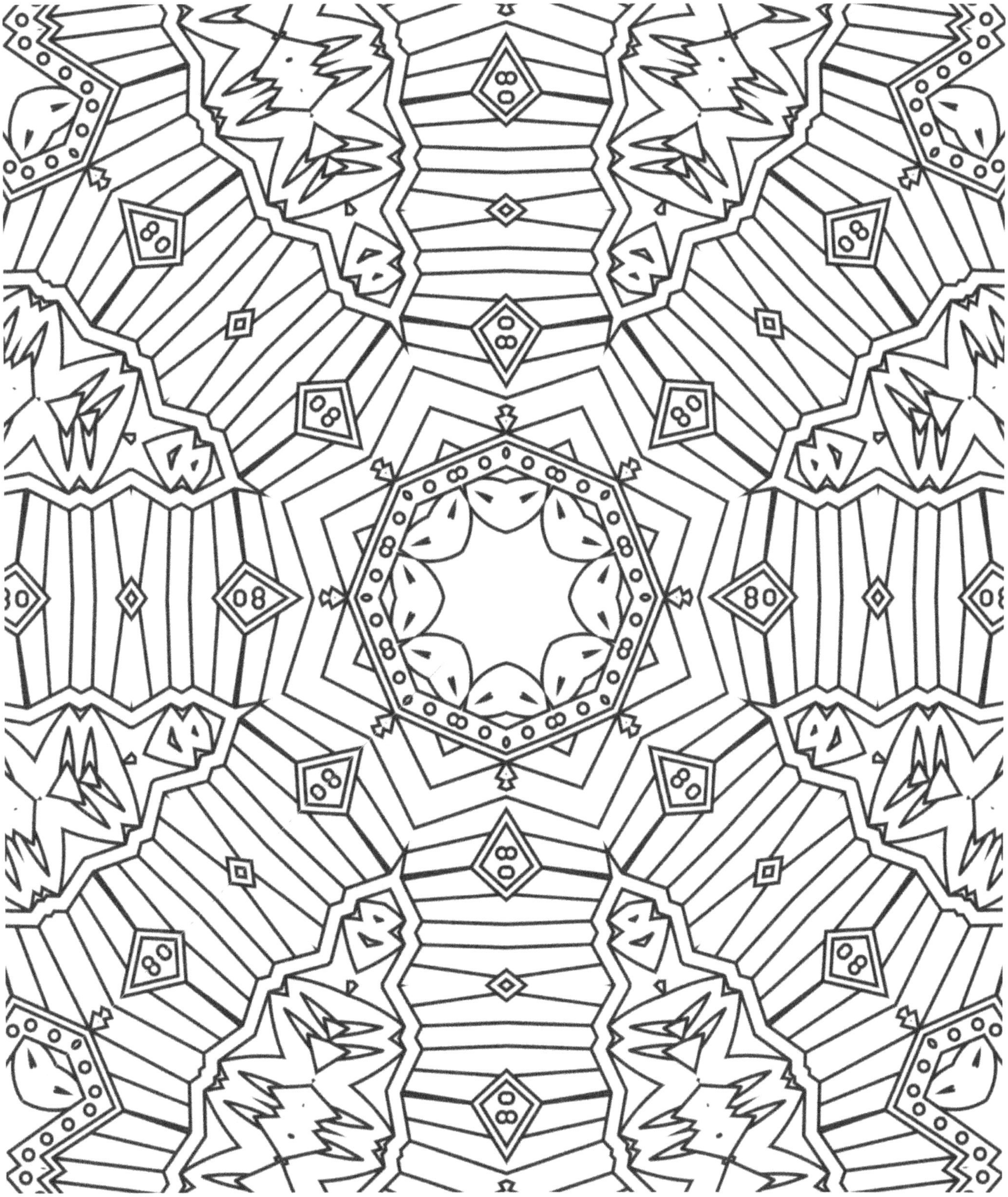

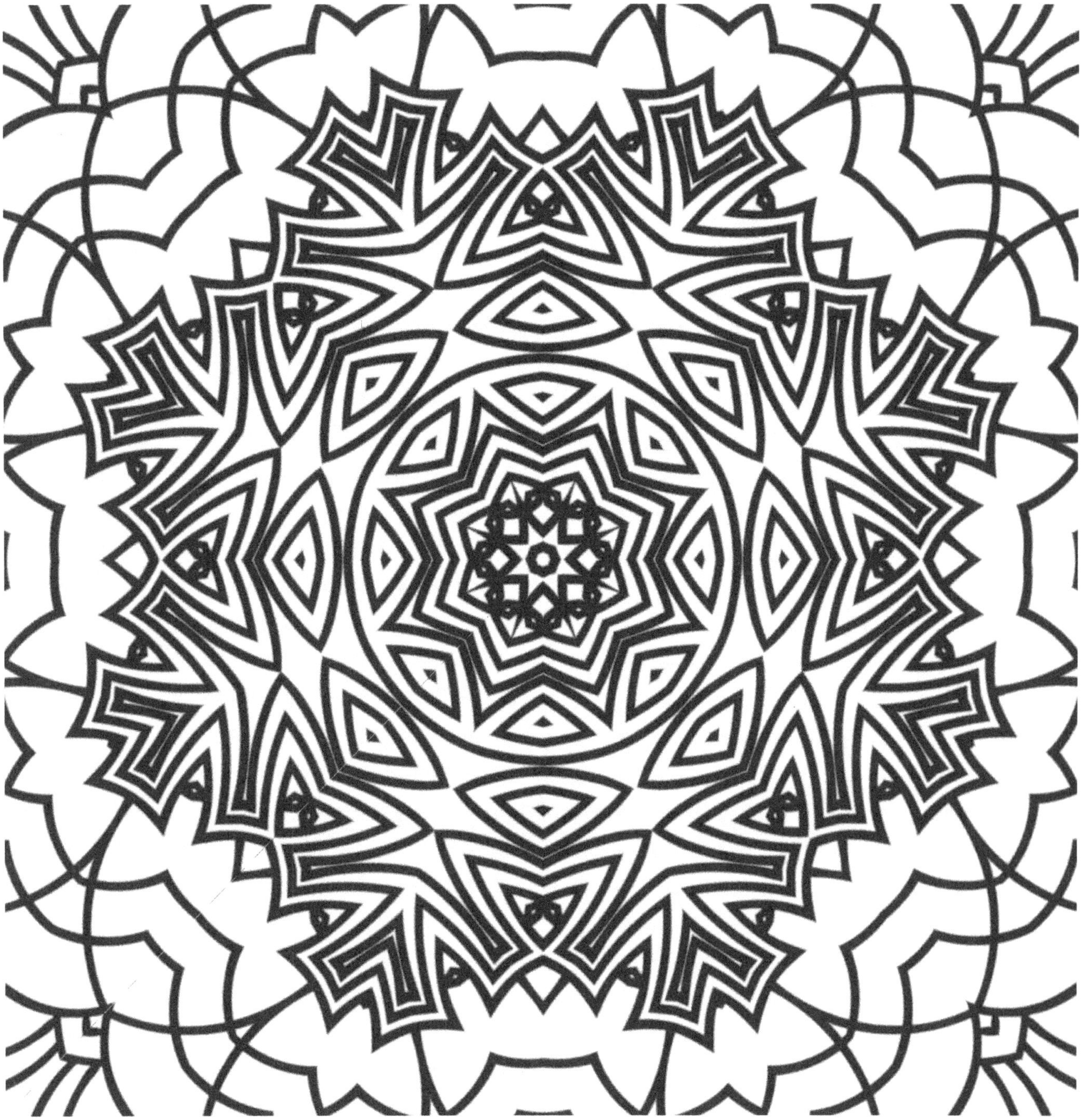

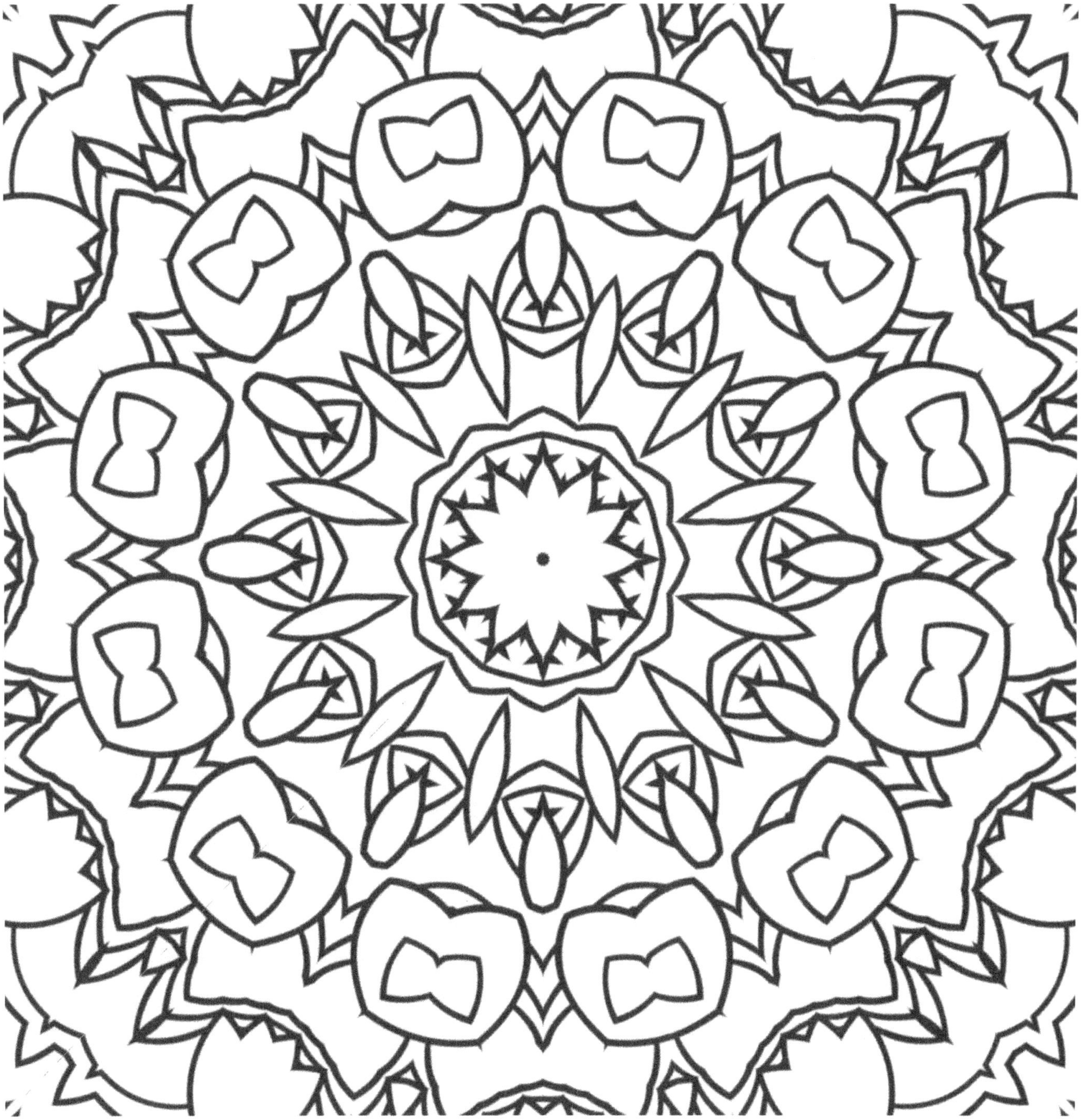

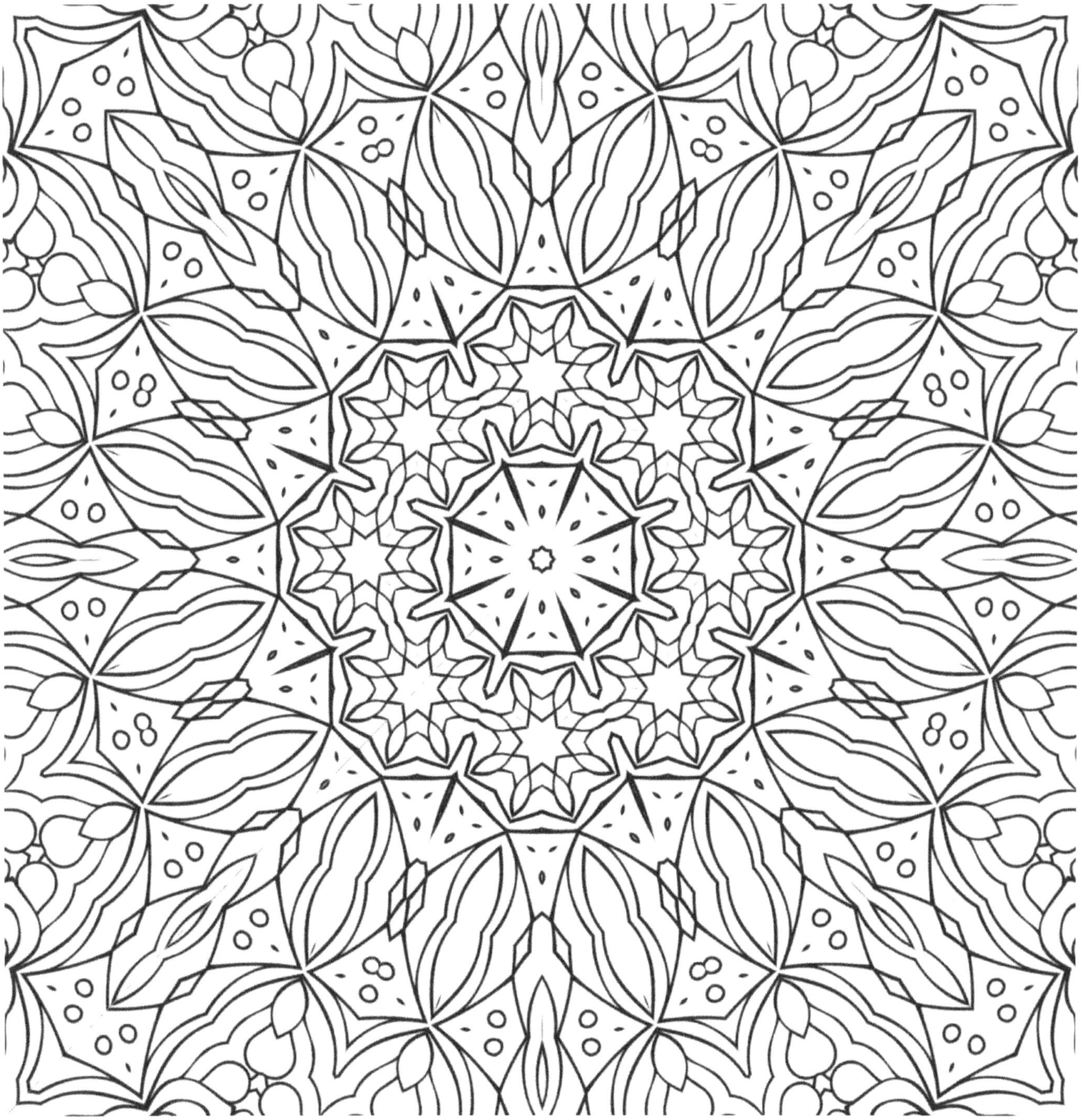

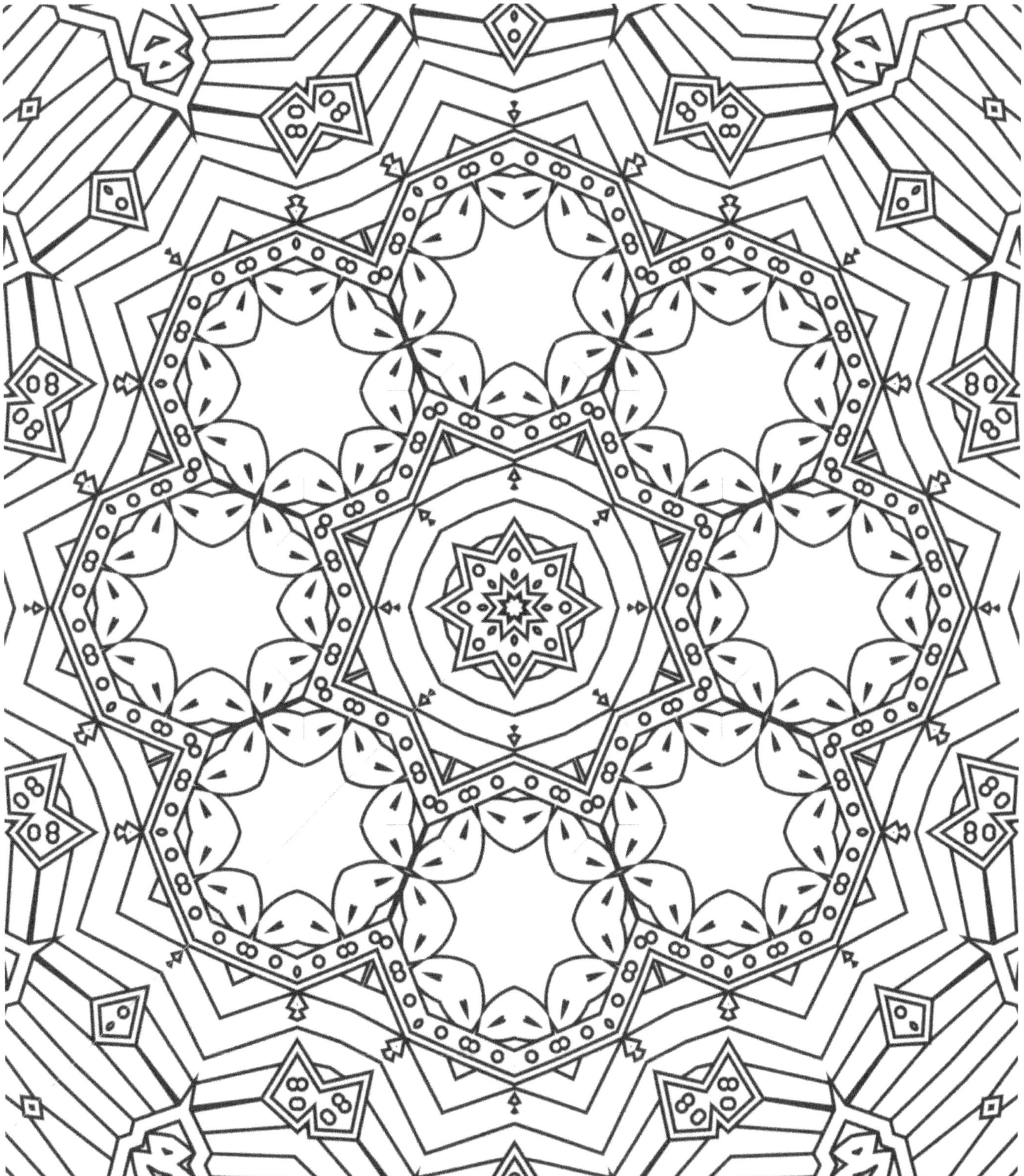

Hope you enjoy this coloring book.

Thank you.

www.ingramcontent.com/pod-product-compliance
Lightning Source LLC
Chambersburg PA
CBHW080832180526
45168CB00006B/2660
9781516927975